Peterson
First Guide

to

DINOSAURS

John C. Kricher

Illustrated by
Gordon Morrison

HOUGHTON
MIFFLIN
COMPANY

•

BOSTON
1990

Library of Congress Cataloging-in-Publication Data

Kricher, John C.
Peterson first guide to dinosaurs.

Summary: Introduces the names and characteristics
of dinosaurs, along with recent discoveries that shed
new light on the way dinosaurs may have lived.
1. Dinosaurs —
Juvenile literature. [1. Dinosaurs].
I. Morrison, Gordon, ill.   II. Title.
QE862.D5K65   1990
567.9'1   89-26697
ISBN 0-395-52440-7

Printed in Italy
NIL   10   9   8   7   6   5   4   3   2   1

Editor's Note

In 1934, my *Field Guide to the Birds* first saw the light of day. This book was designed so that live birds could be readily identified at a distance, by their patterns, shapes, and field marks, without resorting to the technical points specialists use to name species in the hand or in the specimen tray. The book introduced the "Peterson System," as it is now called, a visual system based on patternistic drawings with arrows to pinpoint the key field marks. The system is now used throughout the Peterson Field Guide Series, which has grown to over thirty volumes on a wide range of subjects, from ferns to fishes, rocks to stars, animal tracks to edible plants. Of course, you are not going to see a dinosaur in the field, but the Peterson System is just as useful for learning about extinct creatures as it is for recognizing living ones. Dinosaurs give us an exciting glimpse into the past history of our planet, and the mystery of their sudden extinction can teach us to value more highly the extraordinary animals and plants with which we share today's earth.

Even though Peterson Field Guides are intended for the novice as well as the expert, there are still many beginners who would like something simpler to start with—a smaller guide that would give them confidence. It is for this audience—those who perhaps recognize a crow or robin, buttercup or daisy, but little else—that the Peterson First Guides have been created. They offer a selection of the animals and plants you are most likely to see during your first forays afield. By narrowing the choices—and using the Peterson System—they make identification much easier. First Guides make it easy to get started in the field, and easy to graduate to the full-fledged Peterson Field Guides.

Roger Tory Peterson

Introducing the Dinosaurs

No one has ever seen a living dinosaur. It may seem odd to write a field guide to identification of a group of creatures that have been extinct for millions of years. However, dinosaurs are in the public eye more today than at any other time since their discovery in the early 19th century, just over 150 years ago. The world's great natural history museums, where dinosaur remains are on display, are attracting ever more visitors, curious about the immense reptiles.

It is a romantic notion to hope that somewhere on the planet, in some as yet unexplored forest or swamp, living dinosaurs still persist. Alas, the evidence points otherwise. It has been 65 million years since dinosaurs died out and were replaced by the ancestors of animals we now share our world with. The world of the dinosaurs is a lost world, but we do have their remains to inspire us as we contemplate them. We can study their bones, and infer how they moved from the structure of their skeletons as well as from their fossilized tracks. Some dinosaurs could run fast, or even gallop, like modern mammals. Some could rear up on their hind legs. Some held their tails stiffly, while others had whiplike tails, which they may have used to knock a would-be predator off balance.

By studying their skulls and teeth, we have learned that most dinosaurs ate plants, but some devoured flesh. The width of their ribcages has given us clues to the position of their internal organs — even an idea as to the size of their hearts. The position of their nostrils and the structure of their nasal passages have given us hints about the sounds dinosaurs might have made.

By comparing dinosaur skeletons with those of modern reptiles, birds, and mammals, we can make educated guesses about their anatomy, movement, metabolism, digestion, reproduction, hunting behavior, and social lives. We can also hypothesize about what colors they might have been. Dinosaurs inhabiting deeply shaded forests may have had diamondlike patterning, as snakes such as pythons do. The

4

largest dinosaurs were somewhat similar anatomically to elephants and rhinos, and perhaps they were darkly pigmented, like their mammalian counterparts. Some dinosaurs may have been strongly countershaded (light below, dark above) or have had stripes or other patterning that would have camouflaged them. Some dinosaurs may have had colorful stripes or patterns on the head or body. As in other animals, this may have helped them intimidate rivals or attract mates.

Today, the only places where we can "watch" dinosaurs are museums, libraries, or special parks where dinosaur fossils have been discovered and preserved. By observing dinosaur reconstructions in such museums as the American Museum of Natural History, the Smithsonian Institution, the Field Museum of Natural History in Chicago, or the Royal Ontario Museum in Toronto, you can appreciate firsthand the diversity and size of these unique creatures. By visiting places such as Dinosaur Provincial Park in Alberta, Canada, or Dinosaur National Monument in Utah, you can see dinosaur fossils still embedded in rock in places where dinosaurs lived so many millions of years ago. And by studying the way modern-day reptiles, birds, and mammals live, you can make comparisons to the way dinosaurs probably lived. When you look at the reconstructed skeletons of dinosaurs, take this book along and check off the dinosaurs you see on display. Read about each one as you look at it, and think of how it might have looked with muscle and flesh, and how it might have run, leaped, bellowed, or roared.

In this book dinosaurs are put in the context of the entire geologic history of life on earth. Each of the major groups of dinosaurs is included, along with some other creatures, such as the flying pterosaurs and aquatic plesiosaurs, that were not dinosaurs but lived on earth at the same time.

Dinosaurs were present on earth for approximately 150 million years, during a time called the Mesozoic Era, or "Age of Middle Life." The Mesozoic Era (MEZ-oh-ZOE-ick) is divided into three periods, the Triassic, Jurassic, and

Cretaceous. The Triassic Period (try-AS-sick) began about 225 million years ago, and dinosaurs evolved sometime during the early Triassic. The Jurassic Period (joo-RAS-sick) began 193 million years ago and lasted until the Cretaceous Period (kreh-TAY-shus), which began 136 million years ago. It was during the Jurassic and Cretaceous periods that dinosaurs became the dominant terrestrial (land-dwelling) animals of the time. All dinosaurs became extinct at the close of the Cretaceous Period or very shortly thereafter, about 65 million years ago.

It is tempting to view dinosaurs as "failures" because all of them have become extinct. Such a view is mistaken. Primates, the mammal group to which humans belong, have been on the planet for barely 60 million years, less than half the timespan of the dinosaurs. The apes, to which humans are most closely related, have existed for only 35 million years, not quite one-fourth the time dinosaurs roamed the earth. Our most immediate ancestors, the australopithecines, are only about three and a half million years old. Finally, our species, *Homo sapiens,* is at most a mere hundred thousand years old. Dinosaurs occupied prominent roles on earth for about 1,500 times longer than humans have to date! Successful survival for so many years certainly should not be considered a failure.

Dinosaurs may even still exist, in a manner of speaking. Scientists who have recently studied fossils of the earliest bird, *Archaeopteryx,* have found a very close link between this bird and a group of small, carnivorous (meat-eating) dinosaurs. Many scientists now believe that birds evolved directly from dinosaurs. In their view, today's birds are really feathered dinosaurs, combing the trees for insects, cracking seeds at our bird feeders, and soaring high above us. If this view is correct, our national bird, the Bald Eagle, is also our national dinosaur.

Dinosaur Classification
Dinosaurs were reptiles, though they were very different from snakes, lizards, and other rep-

tiles living today. The word "dinosaur" was coined in the 19th century by a scientist named Richard Owen, who helped describe some of the first dinosaurs ever discovered. Dinosaur means "terrible lizard," a name Owen based on the immense sizes of the newly unearthed creatures.

Not all dinosaurs were huge. Some, even when fully grown, were barely as large as a chicken. However, many were indeed behemoths. In general, dinosaurs were much larger than the largest terrestrial animals of today. The lions, cheetahs, antelopes, buffalo, rhinos, and even the elephants of the African plains are considerably smaller than most of the dinosaurs of similar habits that lived on the plains during the Mesozoic Era. However, the largest animal ever known to exist, the female Blue Whale, with a length of just over 100 ft. and weighing up to 160 tons, is a mammal, not a dinosaur, and is alive today. Whales, of course, live in the oceans, where the water helps support their bulk. The significance of the dinosaurs was that most of them were such large land-dwelling animals.

There were two major groups of dinosaurs. One group, the *saurischians*, (sawr-ISH-she-ans), or lizard-hipped dinosaurs, had hip bones arranged similarly to those of modern lizards. This group contained both plant eaters and meat eaters. The huge sauropods (p. 52), with their long necks and tiny heads, were all herbivores (plant eaters), but the theropods (p. 30), which stood upright and included the immense *Tyrannosaurus rex* (p. 38), the slender ostrich dinosaurs (p. 50), and the small but ferocious coelurosaurs (p. 28), were all carnivores (meat eaters). The other major dinosaur group, the *ornithischians* (OAR-nih-THISH-she-ans), or bird-hipped dinosaurs, had hip bones arranged somewhat like those of modern birds. All of the bird-hipped dinosaurs were herbivorous, surviving entirely on a diet of plants. Included in this group are the stegosaurs (p. 62), ornithopods (p. 64), ankylosaurs (p. 82), and ceratopsids (p. 86).

How Dinosaurs May Have Lived

The earliest reconstructions of dinosaurs showed them as active animals, similar to modern mammals. However, that view soon was replaced by one based more on comparisons of dinosaurs with today's reptiles, the turtles, snakes, lizards, and crocodiles. Dinosaurs were pictured as sprawling, lumbering brutes, some of which were so large that they had to remain in water just to support their huge bodies. Because reptiles are *ectothermic*, or cold-blooded, they cannot maintain a high internal body temperature, and they are often sluggish, especially when the temperature outside is cool. The size of the dinosaurs, combined with the presumption that they functioned internally like lizards and crocodiles, gave rise to the belief that they lived "slow-motion" lives.

In recent years, dinosaurs have been given a new lease on life. Scientists who study dinosaur anatomy (body structure) have discovered some striking similarities between dinosaurs and modern mammals. After examining dinosaur bones under a microscope and studying the places where groups of dinosaur bones have been found, some scientists have concluded that many dinosaurs lived together in communities, and that some dinosaurs may have been warm-blooded animals. If dinosaurs were *endothermic*, or warm-blooded, like birds and mammals, their ability to maintain a high rate of metabolism would have made it possible for them to lead more active lives.

The new view is that dinosaurs lived their lives much more like birds and mammals than like snakes and crocodiles. Instead of moving slowly and resting in the sun to soak up warmth, dinosaurs may have hunted in packs, chasing down prey. They may have had elaborate courtship behaviors, like today's birds. Because of discoveries of fossilized bones and eggs, scientists believe that some dinosaurs lived in colonies, tending their young long after hatching. No longer regarded as lumbering anatomical oddities, dinosaurs are now seen as sleeker, faster, and far more maneuverable than was previously believed. Although discoveries of fossilized dinosaur skin suggest that most dinosaurs probably had scaly or crocodile-like skin, some dinosaurs, especially the smaller ones, may have been covered by feathers, an aid in remaining warm. The link between dinosaurs and birds (all of which are warm-blooded) is very strong.

BIRD-
HIPPED
DINOSAUR

LIZARD-
HIPPED
DINOSAUR

10

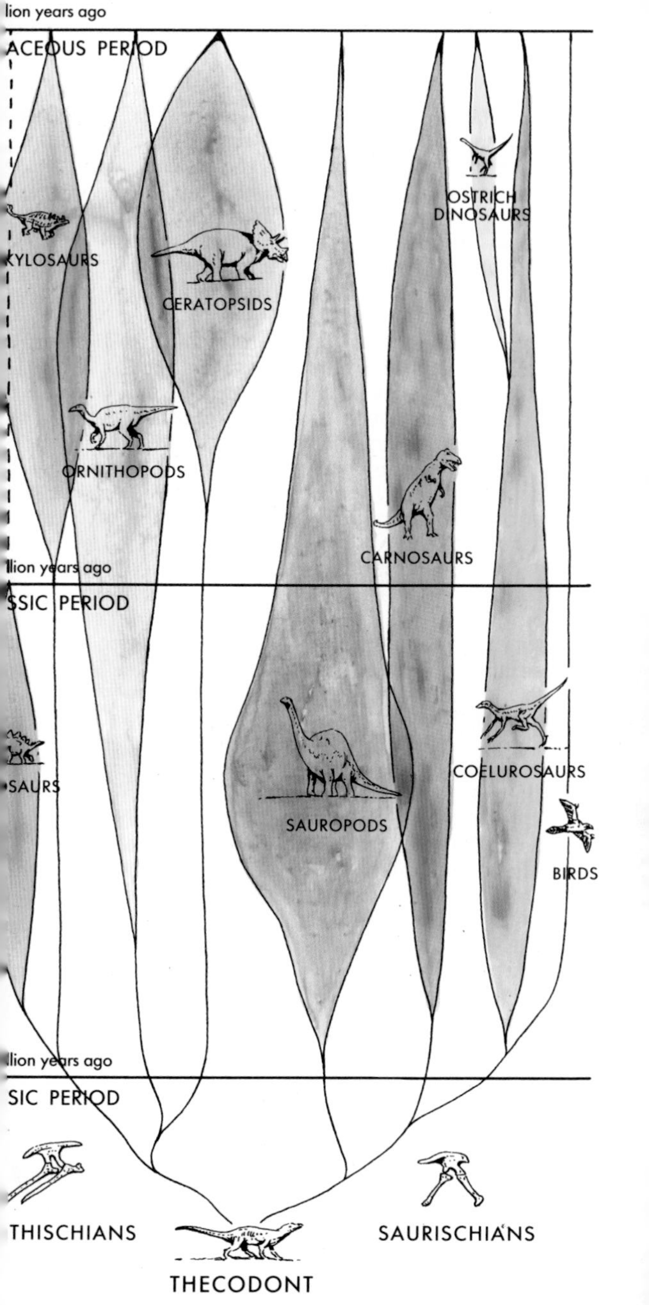

lion years ago
ACEOUS PERIOD

OSTRICH
DINOSAURS

KYLOSAURS

CERATOPSIDS

ORNITHOPODS

CARNOSAURS

llion years ago
SSIC PERIOD

SAUROPODS

COELUROSAURS

SAURS

BIRDS

llion years ago
SIC PERIOD

THISCHIANS

THECODONT

SAURISCHIANS

Geologic Time

Earth has a long history, which began when the planet formed about four and one-half billion years ago. Living organisms, quite similar in many respects to today's bacteria, were present nearly three and one-half billion years ago. However, complex plant and animal life is much more recent, having evolved in the sea less than a billion years ago. Later, some early plants and animals washed ashore and some established themselves on land.

Scientists called paleontologists (PAIL-ee-on-TAHL-oh-jists) are geological historians. They study rocks that date back millions of years. These rocks contain fossils (remains or imprints of remains) that are records of life in the past. Using special techniques of chemistry and geology, paleontologists can date rocks and thus establish how life has changed through time.

Geologists and paleontologists recognize that major changes have periodically occurred on earth, and thus they divide the earth's history into large chunks of time called eras and smaller chunks of time called periods. Though the planet is four and one-half billion years old, animal and plant life has only existed in significant numbers for 600 million years.

From 600 million years ago to the present there have been three geologic eras, named the Paleozoic (which means "ancient life"), Mesozoic ("middle life"), and Cenozoic ("recent life"). The Paleozoic (PAIL-ee-oh-ZOE-ick) consisted of six periods, the Mesozoic (MEZ-oh-ZOE-ick) of three periods, and the Cenozoic (SEE-no-ZOE-ick) of two periods. We are still in the Cenozoic.

Dinosaurs lived during the Mesozoic Era, often called the "Age of Reptiles." Giant dinosaurs walked the earth and huge aquatic reptiles swam in the seas. Mammals evolved in the Triassic Period and birds evolved in the Jurassic. The first flowering plants appeared and insects proliferated in the Cretaceous Period (see p. 18). The Mesozoic Era probably ended with a dramatic cosmic event (see p. 104).

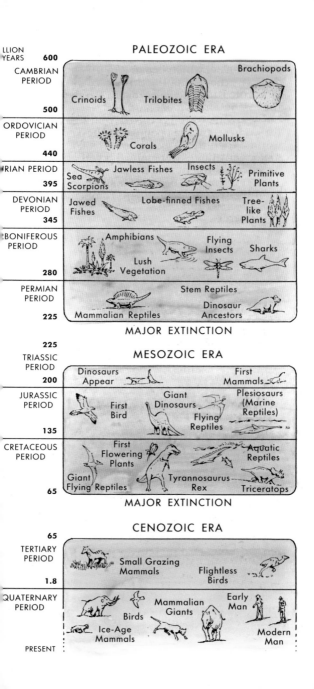

MILLION YEARS

PALEOZOIC ERA

600

CAMBRIAN PERIOD

Brachiopods

Crinoids   Trilobites

500

ORDOVICIAN PERIOD

Corals   Mollusks

440

SILURIAN PERIOD

Sea Scorpions   Jawless Fishes   Insects   Primitive Plants

395

DEVONIAN PERIOD

Jawed Fishes   Lobe-finned Fishes   Tree-like Plants

345

CARBONIFEROUS PERIOD

Amphibians   Flying Insects   Sharks

Lush Vegetation

280

PERMIAN PERIOD

Stem Reptiles

Dinosaur Ancestors

Mammalian Reptiles

225

MAJOR EXTINCTION

225

MESOZOIC ERA

TRIASSIC PERIOD

Dinosaurs Appear   First Mammals

200

JURASSIC PERIOD

First Bird   Giant Dinosaurs   Plesiosaurs (Marine Reptiles)

Flying Reptiles

135

CRETACEOUS PERIOD

First Flowering Plants   Aquatic Reptiles

Giant Flying Reptiles   Tyrannosaurus Rex   Triceratops

65

MAJOR EXTINCTION

CENOZOIC ERA

65

TERTIARY PERIOD

Small Grazing Mammals   Flightless Birds

1.8

QUATERNARY PERIOD

Birds   Mammalian Giants   Early Man

Ice-Age Mammals   Modern Man

PRESENT

Life in the Triassic Period

The Triassic, which began 225 million years ago, was the first of the three periods of the Mesozoic Era. The Paleozoic Era ended with the extinction of most land and sea animals, but many new kinds evolved from their survivors. These animals populated the Triassic world. When the Triassic began, all of the major continents were joined together in a massive continent called Pangaea. During the Triassic, Pangaea began to split apart, initially forming two supercontinents: a northern one

called Laurasia, containing what is now North America, Europe, and northern Asia, and a southern one called Gondwanaland, containing what is now South America, Africa, Antarctica, India, Australia, and parts of southern Asia. This continental drift continues to the present day.

The Triassic world was generally cool and dry. Vast deserts covered much of the interior. Forests of conifers — cone-bearing trees related to pines and spruces — covered the uplands. Along lowland areas, plants called cycads and giant horsetails grew along with ferns. Bulky labyrinthodont amphibians (p. 24), the animals from which the first reptiles evolved, plodded along river banks, but reptiles were becoming the dominant animals by far. Crocodile-like reptiles called phytosaurs (p. 26) inhabited rivers and swamps, along with the first turtles. Swift thecodonts (p. 26), the ancestors of the dinosaurs, scampered along the uplands. Herds of mammal-like reptiles grazed on the cycads and horsetails. By the late Triassic, the archosaurs (p. 26) had given rise to the first dinosaurs and herds of plateosaurs (p. 26) roamed the uplands. Some mammal-like reptiles eventually evolved into true mammals, which were to remain small and inconspicuous for another 125 million years.

15

Life in the Jurassic Period

Throughout the 57 million years of the Jurassic Period, dinosaurs were the dominant land animals. Much of the world's climate was tropical, warm and humid, and upland conifer forests were interspersed with lowland swamps where giant horsetails grew. The continents continued to drift. North America and Europe began to separate, forming the "new" Atlantic Ocean. Gondwanaland was also breaking apart: South America split off from Africa, India moved northward, Antarctica began drifting toward the South Pole, and Australia

moved eastward. Bird-hipped dinosaurs, among them the camptosaurs (p. 70) and plate-backed stegosaurs (p. 62), were abundant. Along with equally abundant herds of immense lizard-hipped dinosaurs called sauropods (p. 52), the bird-hipped dinosaurs fed on varieties of conifers, cycads, and a group of plants called *Bennittitaleans* that resembled palms. Large carnosaurs, among them *Allosaurus* and *Ceratosaurus,* stalked the massive plant eaters. Ichthyosaurs (p. 96) and plesiosaurs (p. 94) snapped up fish in the oceans as crocodiles did in rivers and swamps. Different types of flying reptiles called pterosaurs evolved, and soon shared the skies with true birds. It was in the Jurassic Period that *Archaeopteryx,* the first known bird, evolved, probably from dinosaurs called coelurosaurs (see p. 42). The steamy Jurassic was dominated by the giant reptiles. Mammals continued to evolve, but remained small and inconspicuous.

Life in the Cretaceous Period

During the 71-million-year timespan of the Cretaceous Period the great mountain ranges of the Rockies and Andes formed. A map of the Cretaceous world would more closely resemble a map of the world today, as the separation of the continents was progressing rapidly. Dinosaurs continued to thrive into the mid-Cretaceous Period but then began to decline, becoming totally extinct by the close of the period 65 million years ago.

Among the dinosaurs appeared the bulky ankylosaurs (p. 82) and ceratopsids (p. 86), which were pursued by the huge and ferocious tyrannosaurs. Duck-billed dinosaurs, among them the many kinds of crested dinosaurs called hadrosaurs (p. 74), roamed in vast herds along with various long-necked sauropods (p. 52), browsing on many kinds of trees.

Ginkgos and pines were abundant and familiar trees such as the oaks, magnolias, hickories, dogwoods, and sassafras appeared. These trees and other green plants provided food for dinosaur herds. Flowering plants produced pollen that was fed upon by new kinds of insects, including bees and butterflies. These insects aided in cross-pollinating the new plants, a relationship that continues to the present day. Tall, dark forests of giant

sequoias and redwoods sheltered ostrich dinosaurs (p. 50) and iguanodons (p. 72) as packs
of vicious *Velociraptor* dinosaurs hunted
them. The first grasses appeared.

Seas were habitats for huge sea serpents
called plesiosaurs (p. 94), as well as for fishlike
ichthyosaurs and giant lizards called mosasaurs (p. 92). Bony fishes, much like those
alive today, swam with sharks and giant turtles. Overhead flew the largest of the pterosaurs (p. 98) as well as various ancient birds.
Mammals were lurking inconspicuously in the
underbrush. The world was soon to be dominated by mammals when the great dinosaurs
became extinct.

Fossils

Fossils are the hardened remains of life in the past. Embedded in rocks are bones, teeth, shells, and other parts of ancient creatures. In most cases these parts have become stone, as minerals gradually replaced what was once living tissue.

Fossils are contained in sedimentary rocks, which are made of hardened layers of sediments such as mud and sand. When plants and animals die and become buried in the sediments, they are sometimes preserved within the rock as fossils. As sediments are deposited over time — often on the bottom of a stream, lake, or sea — sedimentary rocks form in layers. The oldest rocks are on the bottom, and the "youngest" ones are on the top. Scientists can look at canyons and other places where layers of rocks have been exposed and see a record of life in long-past ages.

TRILOBITE   To 2 ft.

Trilobites, named for their *three body lobes*, thrived in the ancient oceans. They became extinct before dinosaurs evolved. Trilobites (TRY-loh-bites) were arthropods, related distantly to horseshoe crabs (see pp. 122–123). Most were only a few inches long. They probably fed on small worms and other animals in the mud.

CRINOID   To 2 ft.

Resembling flowers, crinoids (CRY-noyds) are sometimes called "sea lilies." They are actually animals called echinoderms, named for their spiny skin. Crinoids are related to sea stars and sea urchins. They use their *flowerlike tentacles* to capture tiny animals for food. Some crinoids still exist in the deep oceans.

EURYPTERID   To 8 ft.

Called "sea scorpions," these arthropods were probably the first animals that preyed on fishes. Most eurypterids (you-RIP-teh-rids) were small, but some were real giants. All were extinct before the dinosaurs.

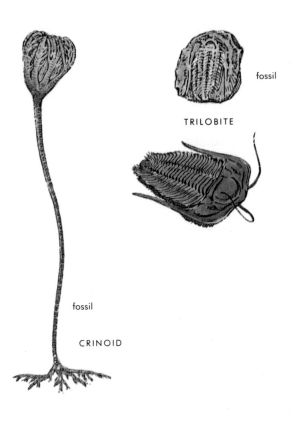

TRILOBITE

fossil

fossil

CRINOID

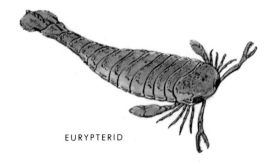

EURYPTERID

Before Dinosaurs

Dinosaurs were vertebrates, animals with backbones. Because of this characteristic, they were related to all other backboned animals, including ourselves. The earliest vertebrates were small jawless fishes that evolved early in the Paleozoic.

OSTRACODERM To 12 in.

Ostracoderm (os-TRACK-oh-derm) means "bone skin," an apt description of these small fishes, the first vertebrates. Their heads were densely covered with *bony armor.* Most ostracoderms were the size of aquarium fish and all were *jawless.* Ostracoderms fed on small worms and other animals they scooped up from the ocean sediments.

PLACODERM To 30 ft.

By the mid-Paleozoic there were many kinds of fishes, including a group called the placoderms (PLACK-oh-derms). These were the first fishes with *jaws.* Placoderms also had *paired fins* and were highly mobile predators. The fish shown here was about the size of a bus! All placoderms were extinct by the end of the Paleozoic.

SHARKS To 50 ft.

Sharks are supported entirely by flexible cartilage (the material we have in our ears), not hard bone. The first sharks date back nearly 400 million years. Sharks that were virtually identical to modern species lived at the same time as the dinosaurs. The shark illustrated is an extinct species of great white shark that may have exceeded 50 ft. in length.

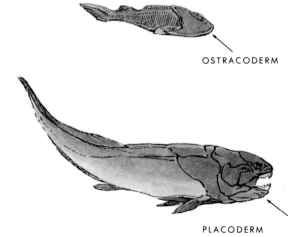

OSTRACODERM

PLACODERM

SHARK

tooth

LOBE-FINNED FISHES   To 2 ft.

These fishes, called sarcopterygians (sahr-COP-teh-RIJ-ee-ans), had a bony skeleton and strong bones and muscles supporting their *front and hind fins.* They could drag themselves over land. They also could gulp and breathe air using a primitive lung. They lived in stagnant ponds and may have moved from pond to pond, breathing air as they did so. Their skull bones and teeth are virtually identical to those of the first amphibians. Paleontologists think amphibians must have evolved from these lobe-finned fishes. Lobe-fins lived in the mid-Paleozoic. Their nearest relatives today are the lungfish and the coelocanth (see pp. 124—125).

LABYRINTHODONT AMPHIBIANS   To 6 ft.

This group of animals was named for its *labyrinthlike tooth structure,* which links the group to the lobe-finned fishes. These bulky, alligator-like amphibians are a far cry from the small, slimy salamanders and frogs of today. Labyrinthodonts (LAB-eh-RINTH-oh-dahnts) thrived during the late Paleozoic Era, feeding on other amphibians and fishes. One group of labyrinthodonts gave rise to a group of early reptiles called stem reptiles.

STEM REPTILES   To 10 ft.

Reptiles, also called cotylosaurs (ko-TILL-oh-sawrs), differ from amphibians in that they lay eggs on land, and thus are freed from the need to be near water in order to reproduce. Reptiles were able to spread out and become established in many landscapes that were uninhabited by amphibians. The stem reptiles are so-called because they gave rise to all other kinds of reptiles, including dinosaurs. Some stem reptiles were only a foot or so in length, but others, like the one shown here, were easily the size of oxen. Their legs *sprawled outward* and they probably moved with a waddle. Some were predators, and many, like this one, were plant eaters.

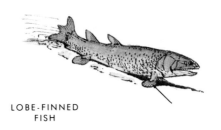

LOBE-FINNED FISH

LABYRINTHODONT AMPHIBIAN

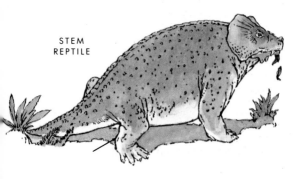

STEM REPTILE

Dinosaur Ancestors

The ancestors of dinosaurs were reptiles called *archosaurs* (AR-koh-sawrs). These reptiles evolved about 225 million years ago. Most were small, about 3 ft. long, and many were aquatic. Some bore striking similarities to crocodiles.

THECODONT   To 10 ft.

Thecodonts (THEE-koh-dahnts), which thrived during the Triassic Period, were ancestors to all dinosaurs. Their name means "teeth in sockets," a characteristic they shared with dinosaurs. Some, like *Euparkeria* (YOU-park-AIR-ee-uh), illustrated here, resembled the larger carnivorous dinosaurs of the future.

PHYTOSAUR   To 15 ft.

Phytosaurs (FY-toh-sawrs), which look almost identical to crocodiles, evolved from aquatic thecodonts. They differed from crocodiles in that their nostrils were located near the eyes *at the base* of the snout, not at the tip, like crocodile nostrils. They became extinct shortly after crocodiles evolved. The name phytosaur means "plant lizard," a mistake, because all phytosaurs ate meat.

PLATEOSAURUS   To 20 ft.

One of the first of the lizard-hipped dinosaurs, *Plateosaurus* (PLAT-tih-oh-SAW-rus) roamed through what is now Germany and France just over 200 million years ago. Plateosaurs are thought to be the ancestors of the huge brontosaurs and their relatives (see p. 52). Note the similarity in body structure to the thecodonts.

THECODONT

PHYTOSAUR

PLATEOSAURUS

Carnivorous Dinosaurs

One major branch of the saurischian (lizard-hipped) dinosaurs was entirely composed of meat-eating species. This diverse group consisted of small and medium-sized birdlike dinosaurs as well as the largest carnivores ever to roam the earth. One group probably gave rise to the birds.

Early Coelurosaurs

The coelurosaurs (see-LOOR-oh-saurs) were a group of small, agile carnivores that evolved in the late Triassic. Different types developed and persisted through the late Cretaceous. These dinosaurs were rather like miniature streamlined tyrannosaurs. They have been called the jackals and hyenas of their time. Most had *long necks and tails,* with forelimbs that were useful for *grasping.* Coelurosaurs ranged in size from 2 to 18 ft. Some may have been even larger.

COELOPHYSIS   To 10 ft.

This 65-pound dinosaur (pronounced SEE-loh-FY-sis) was the wolf of the late Triassic. In a remote place in New Mexico called Ghost Ranch, numerous skeletons of adults and young have been excavated. The teeth discovered there were *sharp and serrated.* These little dinosaurs may have hunted in packs. There is also evidence that some may have killed and eaten young of the species.

HERRERASAURUS   To 12 ft.

The herrerasaurs (her-AIR-uh-sawrs) lived during the late Triassic. Fossils have been found in Europe, Africa, and South America. Several fine fossils have come from Argentina. Though herrerasaurs were among the earliest of the dinosaurs, some developed a body structure much like that of the larger carnosaurs that would follow. These dinosaurs were swift runners, with *large, powerful hind limbs.* Their forelimbs, like those of other predatory dinosaurs, were small.

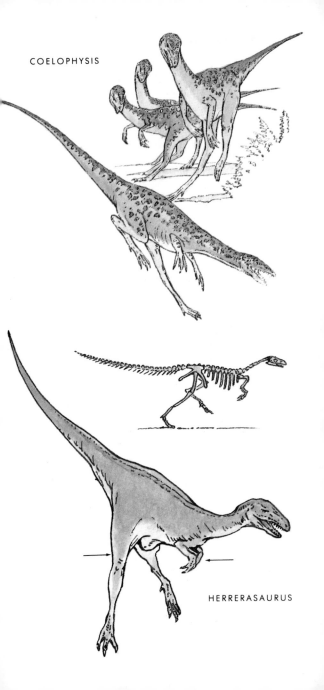

COELOPHYSIS

HERRERASAURUS

Theropod Carnosaurs

Theropods are one of the two groups of saurischians, or lizard-hipped dinosaurs. Carnosaurs (CAR-no-sawrs), one of the major kinds
of theropods, were the lions and tigers of the
dinosaur world. These *bipedal (upright)* dinosaurs were generally large. All of them were
meat eaters. They pursued their prey by running on their strong hind legs. At full speed,
the body was held nearly horizontal, and the
stiff tail helped balance the beast. The *small
forelimbs* were probably used to tear apart
prey after the kill. Carnosaurs had *large skulls*
lined with *sharp, often serrated teeth,* ideal for
killing and ripping apart flesh.

CERATOSAURUS   To 20 ft.

This dinosaur was unusual among carnosaurs for the *odd hornlike projection* on its
nose. *Ceratosaurus* (SEER-a-toe-SAW-rus)
lived in North America during the late Jurassic Period.

ALLOSAURUS   To 39 ft.

Perhaps the largest carnosaur of the Jurassic Period, a mature allosaur (AL-oh-sawr)
could weigh up to 4 tons. Its fearsome head
was held 15 ft. above the ground. It probably hunted large sauropods. Teeth were serrated on both sides, and were housed in a
skull that measured a *yard in length!* This
dinosaur was from western North America.

DILOPHOSAURUS   To 20 ft.

This carnosaur is notable both for its odd
double crest atop the head and for its *jaw
structure,* which was much weaker than
that of most carnosaurs. *Dilophosaurus*
(DIE-loh-foh-SAW-rus) lived early in the Jurassic, long before the allosaurs evolved.

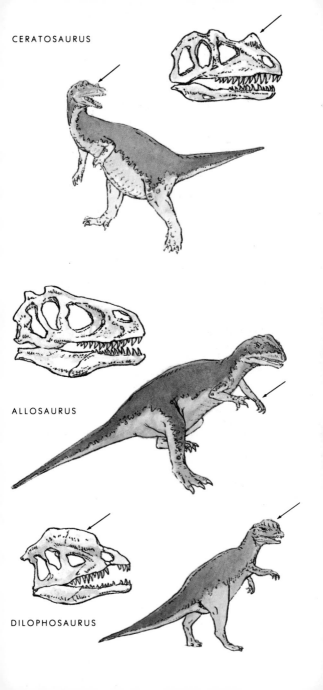

CERATOSAURUS

ALLOSAURUS

DILOPHOSAURUS

METRIACANTHOSAURUS To 30 ft.

This carnosaur of the late Jurassic was recently excavated in Sichuan, China. In many ways it closely resembled *Ceratosaurus* (see p. 31), though it lacked the prominent hornlike structure on the snout. Its head ornaments were similar to those found on *Allosaurus* (see p. 31), with *small horns* above each eye and *two bony ridges* on the face. *Metriacanthosaurus* (meh-TREE-ah-can-tho-SAW-rus) probably preyed on large sauropods and stegosaurs.

CARNOTOSAURUS To 20 ft.

One of the most recently discovered dinosaurs, *Carnotosaurus* (car-NO-tah-SAW-rus) lived in what is now Argentina during the early Cretaceous Period. Its skull had *two prominent bony horns,* one over each eye. Perhaps these dinosaurs engaged in battles for territories or mates by butting horns together. In addition to a fossilized skeleton, skin impressions have been found that indicate the dinosaur was covered with rows of large scales.

METRIACANTHOSAURUS

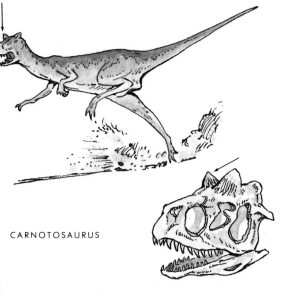

CARNOTOSAURUS

MEGALOSAURUS To 30 ft.

Fossils of this carnosaur of the mid-Jurassic were first discovered and described in 1824, only two years after the discovery of the first dinosaur fossils was announced (see pp. 72–73). The original fossil of *Megalosaurus* (MEG-gah-loh-SAW-rus) consisted only of part of the lower jawbone (with teeth), and came from Oxford, England. The teeth were so impressively large that the total length of the animal was estimated to be 40 ft., much longer than the actual length that was determined from more complete fossils later. The first restorations of this dinosaur include an impressive full-scale sculpture that can still be seen in south London on the grounds of the old Crystal Palace, built for the Great Exhibition of 1851. This restoration shows the animal rather like a rhinoceros, on all fours. Only later, when far more complete skeletons were unearthed, were the true shape and size of this dinosaur realized.

Megalosaurus skeletons have been found in the United States, Australia, Europe, Africa, and India. The wide distribution of these fossils provides support for the belief that the continents were tightly connected during the Jurassic. Certainly these land-dwelling dinosaurs could never have crossed oceans to reach the continents if these land masses had been in their present positions.

early
restoration

MEGALOSAURUS

ALBERTOSAURUS   To 30 ft.

This carnosaur of the late Cretaceous was a small version of *Tyrannosaurus* (see next page). This dinosaur, formerly named *Gorgosaurus*, weighed only 2 tons instead of 6 or 7. This large but limber predator hunted prey in western North America. It actually had more teeth than *Tyrannosaurus*. The *saberlike teeth* curved backward and were sharpened on both sides, a useful feature for slashing flesh. Like most of the giant carnosaurs, *Albertosaurus* had *small abdominal ribs* that helped support its bulk when resting on the ground. *Albertosaurus* had *very small arms*, each of which had only two fingers. It is doubtful that these arms were of much use in manipulating prey. *Tyrannosaurus* had even smaller arms.

ALBERTOSAURUS

TYRANNOSAURUS REX   To 40 ft.

This amazing dinosaur of the late Cretaceous Period is the largest terrestrial predator ever known to exist. It stood almost 20
ft. tall, and its skull alone was just over *4 ft.
long.* A single tyrannosaur tooth is 7 in.
long. The teeth curved backward and were
serrated on both sides. The animal weighed
nearly 7 tons, as much as a large African
elephant. Although it was huge, the brain of
a tyrannosaur was actually smaller than the
animal's largest tooth! This dinosaur could
run swiftly on *powerful hind legs,* using its
muscular tail as a counterbalance. Each
hind foot had three strong toes pointing for-
ward and one small toe pointing to the rear,
as on the foot of a modern rooster. The
arms were *very small* and probably useless.

Some scientists believe tyrannosaurs
were mostly scavengers, but most scientists
think that they were savage carnivores that
fed on such dinosaurs as *Triceratops* (see
pp. 88–89). Remains of tyrannosaurs come
from western North America and China.
The first skeleton came from Montana, in a
place appropriately called Hell Creek. The
name *Tyrannosaurus rex* (ty-RAN-oh-SAW-
rus REX) means "king of tyrant lizards." It
certainly was.

TYRANNOSAURUS REX

SPINOSAURUS To 50 ft.

One of the oddest of the dinosaurs, *Spinosaurus* (SPY-no-SAW-rus) is known only from a partial skeleton excavated from late Cretaceous rock in Egypt. Its backbone was composed of vertebrae with *elongated spines* that are thought to have supported a large finlike structure on its upper back. The animal was large, perhaps even longer than *Tyrannosaurus*, though it was more slender and probably weighed less. A piece of its lower jaw was also found. Its teeth were similar to the conical teeth of today's crocodiles.

The function of the unique "fin" on *Spinosaurus* is a mystery. However, two other unrelated species from the mid-Cretaceous Period in north Africa had similar structures. Perhaps these "fins" had a common function. A wide fin of skin, well supplied with blood vessels, could have helped the animal absorb heat when it was cold and radiate heat when it was hot, thus helping it maintain a relatively constant body temperature. Similar structures were found on some ancient mammal-like reptiles that preceded the dinosaurs (see pp. 108–109).

SPINOSAURUS

Later Coelurosaurs

COMPSOGNATHUS   To 2 ft.

This was one of the smallest dinosaurs, barely the size of a chicken. Tiny *Compsognathus* (KOMP-so-NAY-thus) must have pursued insects and very small vertebrates. It also may have eaten eggs. Some scientists believe it may have been warm-blooded and that it may have been covered with feathers or hairlike insulation. It lived in the late Jurassic Period. Its fossils come from West Germany and southern France.

ORNITHOLESTES   To 6½ ft.

This moderate-sized coelurosaur lived in western North America during the late Jurassic. The name *Ornitholestes* (OAR-nith-oh-LES-tees) means "bird robber," a reference to the notion that this dinosaur routinely preyed on birds. It is more likely that *Ornitholestes* hunted smaller dinosaurs and perhaps early mammals. Its teeth were large and its bite powerful, and its *long forelimbs and fingers* indicate that it may have grabbed prey by a quick lunge. *Ornitholestes* probably had a powerful grip.

COMPSOGNATHUS

ORNITHOLESTES

OVIRAPTOR To 6 ft.

This little dinosaur has a name that means "egg stealer." The first fossils of *Oviraptor* (OH-vih-RAP-tor) were found in Outer Mongolia, near the nests of *Protoceratops* (see pp. 84–85). Some people think that *Oviraptor* was killed in a sandstorm while it was stealing eggs. The skull, which is *very short* and almost completely lacking in teeth, was probably covered by a horny sheath. There was also a *horny crest* atop the odd head, giving this small dinosaur a very strange appearance. *Oviraptor* was a swift runner. Its long arms had sharp, *sickle-like claws* that could have been useful for defense.

TROODON To 6½ ft.

This swift, slender dinosaur is sometimes called *Stenonychosaurus* (STEN-oh-NICK-oh-SAW-rus). The first fossils of this dinosaur were unearthed in Mongolia and date from the late Cretaceous. Other *Troodon* (TROW-oh-DON) fossils come from Montana and Alberta, Canada. This dinosaur has been called a "proto-bird," though it hardly resembles today's robins and sparrows. In fact, it existed well after birds evolved (see pp. 48–49). *Troodon* had a large brain (for a dinosaur) and *prominent eyes* with overlapping fields of vision. It may have hunted small mammals at night. This dinosaur has been the subject of speculation about how dinosaurs might have evolved if they had not become extinct. See p. 126.

OVIRAPTOR

TROODON

VELOCIRAPTOR

To 10 ft.

Also called *Deinonychus* (DY-noh-NICK-us), this small dinosaur from western North America lived in the mid-Cretaceous. The name *Deinonychus* means "terrible claw," a reference to the *large curved claw* on the second toe of the hind foot. This claw was jointed, which allowed it to be raised and lowered efficiently. The claw was held above ground as the animal ran and was probably used for slashing, to bring down and dismember prey.

Velociraptor (VELL-oh-sih-RAP-tor), whose name means "swift robber," was probably a vicious little predator that hunted in packs. Though this dinosaur only weighed about 150 pounds and was barely 5 ft. tall, a pack of these swift dinosaurs could have been more than a match for a large sauropod. Their hind legs were long and strong, ideal for running. Their tail was *rigid*, supported by tendons that added strength and stiffness. The anatomy of *Velociraptor* was well suited for speed and high levels of activity. This has convinced some scientists that these dinosaurs were warm-blooded and that they may have even had feathers.

VELOCIRAPTOR

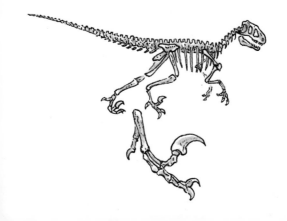

The First Bird

The very first dinosaur tracks discovered in the United States are from the Connecticut Valley. The animals that made them were mistakenly named "Noah's Ravens" because the tracks look so much like those made by birds. Surprisingly, birds share many anatomical similarities with reptiles, especially crocodilians. Scientists now recognize that birds evolved from reptiles in the late Jurassic. The probable ancestor to birds was an early coelurosaur dinosaur. Some scientists argue that birds are indeed modern feathered dinosaurs, and ought to be classified as such.

ARCHAEOPTERYX   To 3 ft.

This is the earliest known bird. Its fossils were found in Bavaria in 1860. If the imprints of the feathers had not been beautifully preserved along with the skeleton, the animal would have been considered a coelurosaur. Unlike modern birds, *Archaeopteryx* (ar-kee-OP-teh-ricks) has a *bony tail*, *clawed fingers*, and jaws with *teeth*. It could fly well and probably lived in open habitats along lakes or seashores.

"PROTO-AVIS"

This is a hypothetical animal, one that has not actually been found yet. It represents an early stage in the development of feathers and flight, the characteristics that distinguish birds. Feathers may have originally evolved to help animals retain heat, assuming that the ancestors of birds were warm-blooded. Flight may have evolved from running to pursue insect prey, or from gliding after climbing a tree. No one knows exactly how or when feathers and flight evolved.

ARCHAEOPTERYX

"PROTO-AVIS"

Ostrich Dinosaurs

As the name implies, these dinosaurs of the late Cretaceous bore a resemblance to ostriches. Related to the coelurosaurs, they were slender, swift carnivores that probably fed on insects, mammals, baby dinosaurs, and dinosaur eggs.

ORNITHOMIMUS To 12 ft.

The name of this dinosaur translates as "bird mimic." *Ornithomimus* (OAR-nith-oh-MY-mus) looked much like a modern ostrich without feathers. Its hind legs were long and strong, capable of running at great speed. Its arms were also *long*, with *three fingers* for manipulating small prey. The eyes were *large* and the jaws *lacked teeth*, making the skull quite birdlike in appearance. *Ornithomimus* stood about 6 ft. tall.

One strange fossil found in Mongolia is named *Deinocheirus* (DY-no-KEER-us), which means "terrible claw." It may have been a gigantic ostrich dinosaur. Only the arms were found. Each has three huge slashing claws, and each arm measures 8½ ft. long!

ring of bones
supporting eye

birdlike skull

ORNITHOMIMUS

arm of
DEINOCHEIRUS

The Huge Sauropods

Sauropods were huge plant eaters of the Jurassic and (to a lesser extent) Cretaceous periods. Many of these dinosaurs would dwarf the largest elephant. They probably lived in herds, foraging on needles from tall conifers, which the sauropods reached with their long necks. When sauropods were first discovered, it was believed that they were too large to stand on land. Scientists thought they lived in swamps and lakes, where their bulk could be "floated" by water. Though sauropods may have cooled their immense bodies by soaking in lakes, their anatomy was more than adequate to support their weight on land. They probably moved quite efficiently, much like modern elephants.

APATOSAURUS   To 70 ft.

Formerly named *Brontosaurus*, this is one of the best-known dinosaurs. *Brontosaurus* means "thunder lizard," an apt name for this huge dinosaur. It probably tipped the scales at about 36 tons (an elephant weighs 3–6 tons). Remains of this dinosaur, which is now called *Apatosaurus* (ay-PAT-oh-SAW-rus), have been found both in Europe and the western United States. Like all large sauropods, *Apatosaurus* had a head that was *small* in relation to its body size. It probably fed by swallowing large quantities of vegetation and grinding it up using a spacious, gizzardlike stomach.

APATOSAURUS

DIPLODOCUS
To 90 ft.

Diplodocus (DIP-loh-DOH-kus) was a slender version of *Apatosaurus,* to which it was closely related. Its neck alone measured 26 ft., and its tail was 45 ft. long, but it probably weighed "only" 12 tons. It may have used its powerful, *whiplike tail* as a defense against large predatory dinosaurs. Its head was somewhat *elongated,* with peglike teeth suitable for snipping vegetation, but not for grinding. *Diplodocus* roamed the western United States during the Jurassic.

CAMARASAURUS
To 60 ft.

This husky sauropod inhabited what is now Colorado and Utah during the Jurassic Period. Its neck and tail were proportionately *shorter* than those of both *Apatosaurus* and *Diplodocus.* The odd *position of the nostrils,* high on the skull, suggested to some that camarasaurs (KAM-ah-rah-sawrs) had elephantine trunks! Recent studies reject this notion, favoring the idea that the large nostrils were highly sensitive to odors or were used to cool the blood. Teeth were *chisel-like,* and quite close together. Camarasaurs probably ate very coarse, tough plants.

nostril

DIPLODOCUS

nasal cavity

claw

nostril

nasal cavity

CAMARASAURUS

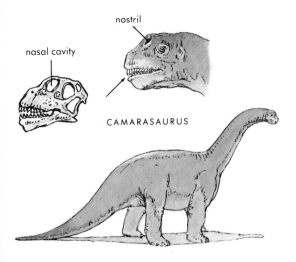

MAMENCHISAURUS To 72 ft.

Inhabiting what is now southern and central China during the late Jurassic Period, *Mamenchisaurus* (MAH-men-kee-SAW-rus) was distinguished by its *extremely long neck*, which contained a total of 19 large vertebrae. The neck alone measured 33 ft., and no other dinosaur had so many neck bones. Modern mammals, including the long-necked giraffe, have only seven. Although the neck was long, it was not very flexible because the vertebrae were interconnected by bony processes. These bones made the neck quite strong but rather stiff. The dinosaur probably fed on vegetation from among the tallest trees, the giant sequoias and redwoods. Vast forests of these trees covered much of the Jurassic landscape. Because of its long neck and skull characteristics, *Mamenchisaurus* is thought by most paleontologists to be a relative of *Diplodocus*, but some scientists believe it is sufficiently distinct that it should be placed in its own family.

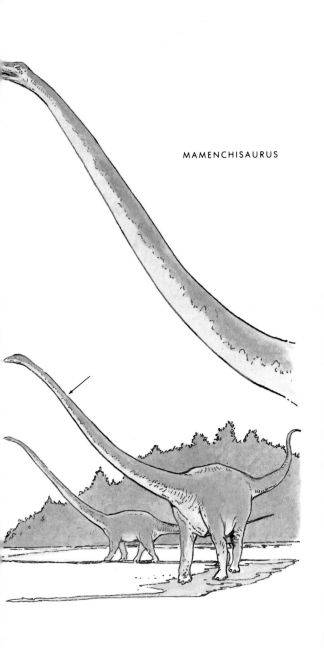

MAMENCHISAURUS

BRACHIOSAURUS

The brachiosaurs, which ranged widely over Europe, Africa, and North America during the late Jurassic and early Cretaceous periods, had the most massive bodies of any dinosaurs. An adult *Brachiosaurus* (BRAY-kee-oh-SAW-rus) weighed about 66 tons! From toes to nostrils, the animal was 40 ft. in height. Unlike most sauropods, brachiosaurs had *longer forelegs* than hind legs, adding to their overall height (the name means "arm-lizard"). Nostrils were positioned *high atop the skull*, leading some to suggest that they served as snorkels, allowing the huge animal to breathe while submersed. This could not be true, because if the dinosaur were 40 ft. deep in water, the water pressure would prevent it from expanding its chest to breathe. Like other sauropods and much like modern giraffes, brachiosaurs probably fed on upland vegetation cropped from tall trees.

Recently fossils have been found in the western United States that suggest creatures similar to but even larger than *Brachiosaurus* existed. One, called *"Supersaurus,"* may have stood 54 ft. tall. Another, called *"Ultrasaurus,"* may have weighed 150 tons, with a length of over 100 ft. Such an animal was tall enough to look into a 6-story building, and would have eaten 5 tons of plant food per day!

nostrils

eye

BRACHIOSAURUS

An Unusual Sauropod

SALTASAURUS To 39 ft.

Many people believe that most dinosaurs have already been discovered. However, part of the excitement that surrounds the study of dinosaurs is that new kinds are still being unearthed, and some of these animals are indeed unique. Such is the case with *Saltasaurus* (SALT-ah-SAW-rus). This rather small sauropod is named for the area in Argentina where it was discovered in 1980.

Judging from its skeleton, *Saltasaurus* was shaped like a rather husky brontosaur, but its bones were found along with remains of what must have been *skin armor.* Apparently this dinosaur was protected by *thick, oval, bony plates* that were scattered among a dense covering of *hardened studs* that projected outward, perhaps resembling the skin of a crocodile. The skeleton of *Saltasaurus*, like that of all sauropods, was quite strong but also rather agile. The dinosaur had a strengthened tail and could probably have stood on its hind legs, using its tail as a prop, somewhat like a massive kangaroo. This could have helped the animal reach tall vegetation. *Saltasaurus* was one of the last of the dinosaurs, living in the late Cretaceous Period.

SALTASAURUS

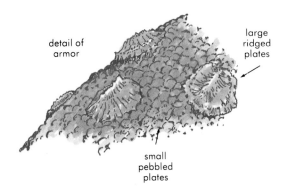

detail of armor

large ridged plates

small pebbled plates

Stegosaurs

Stegosaurs were bird-hipped dinosaurs, most notable for the odd arrangements of *bony plates* that lined their backs. These plates had numerous blood vessels and may have helped the dinosaur gain or lose heat. They may have also helped protect these small-headed plant eaters from the onslaughts of carnosaurs (see p. 30). The stegosaurs' only other defense was their *tail*, often tipped with *long spikes*, which could be thrashed at enemies. Stegosaur brains were very small: in the largest stegosaurs the brain was only about the size of a walnut. Most stegosaurs lived during the Jurassic and all were herbivores.

KENTROSAURUS   To 8 ft.
This small stegosaur had *spikes* running well up its back. Its remains are known only from Tanzania in Africa.

STEGOSAURUS   To 25 ft.
The best known of the stegosaurs, *Stegosaurus* (STEG-oh-SAW-rus) lived among the brontosaurs and allosaurs of western North America. It may have reared up on its hind legs to browse. Scientists are still uncertain about the arrangement of its *large, triangular bony plates*. Some believe they were in two rows; others argue for a single row. Some say the truth is in between, as we show here.

TUOJIANGOSAURUS   To 20 ft.
Stegosaurs roamed widely. This one lived in what is now China. *Tuojiangosaurus* (TOO-yin-go-SAW-rus) had *small bony plates.*

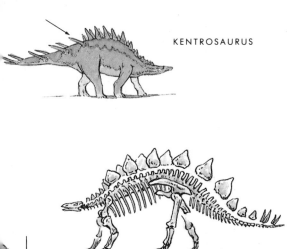

KENTROSAURUS

STEGOSAURUS

TUOJIANGOSAURUS

Ornithopods

Ornithopods were a diverse and abundant group of ornithischians (bird-hipped dinosaurs) that lived over most of the earth during the Jurassic and Cretaceous periods. There were many kinds of ornithopods, but the most prominent were the Cretaceous iguanodonts and hadrosaurs. Ornithopods had large hind legs and could easily rear up. Many were probably bipedal (stood upright), but their arms were strong and may have been used in walking. Ornithopods lived on land and ate only plant material.

Fabrosaurs

The fabrosaurs (FAH-bro-sawrs) were early ornithopods. These small dinosaurs (reaching only 6 ft. in length) also may have been the ancestors of all other bird-hipped or ornithischian dinosaurs. They evolved in the late Triassic Period and persisted through the Jurassic. All were plant eaters, cropping vegetation with *sharp, often serrated teeth* that resembled tiny spearheads.

LESOTHOSAURUS   To 3¼ ft.

This small, fleet dinosaur inhabited what is now southern Africa in the late Triassic.

SCUTELLOSAURUS   To 4½ ft.

This small fabrosaur of the early Jurassic was covered by *bony plates and tubercles*, somewhat like the skin of an alligator, on its upper side. These plates probably served as protection against predators. *Scutellosaurus* (SKEW-tell-oh-SAW-rus) also had a *long tail* and its front legs were not a great deal smaller than its hind legs. It probably moved on all fours but could run fast on its hind legs when the need arose. Fossils have been found in Arizona.

LESOTHOSAURUS

teeth

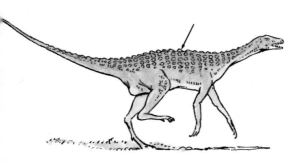

SCUTELLOSAURUS

detail of armor

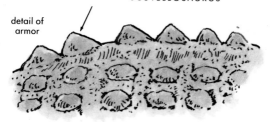

Heterodontosaurs

The rather cumbersome name of this group of early dinosaurs refers to the different types of teeth they had. Like their close relatives, the fabrosaurs, they were swift runners and were probably very agile. Heterodontosaurs (HET-ter-oh-DON-toe-sawrs) lived from the late Triassic through the Jurassic.

HETERODONTOSAURUS To 4 ft.

Heterodontosaurus (HET-ter-oh-DON-toe-SAW-rus), from what is now South Africa, had *three different kinds of teeth — incisors, canines,* and *grinding molars* — with which to nip and chew vegetation. Its lower jaw was probably capable of some side-to-side motion, an aid in chewing fibrous plants.

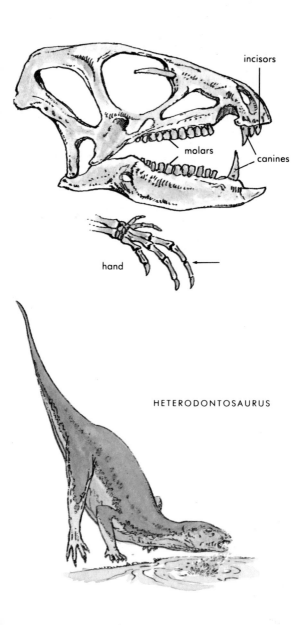

incisors

molars

canines

hand

HETERODONTOSAURUS

Hypsilophodonts

Appearing first in the mid-Jurassic Period and lasting through the Cretaceous, the hypsilophodonts (HIP-sih-LOFF-oh-dahnts) represent a diverse and successful group of plant eaters. They were ornithischians, similar in many respects to fabrosaurs. They were small, ranging in length from about 6 to 16 ft. Their skulls and teeth were well structured for chewing coarse vegetation, and their jaw muscles were powerful. Their teeth were long, close together, and well suited for grinding. A *horny beak* covered the tip of the upper jaw, and was probably helpful in cropping plants. These dinosaurs have been called the gazelles of their time. They had long legs, including an elongated ankle and foot, and could run very swiftly. The tail, *stiffly supported* by tendons, acted as a counterbalance as the animal ran.

HYPSILOPHODON   To 7½ ft.

Hypsilophodon (HIP-sih-LOFF-oh-don) lived in the early Cretaceous and ranged widely. Fossils have been found from North Dakota to England. The anatomy of this dinosaur indicates that it must have been a very swift runner, though early reconstructions mistakenly showed it as a tree dweller!

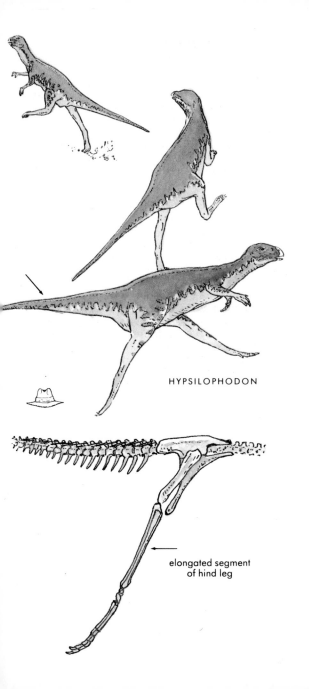

HYPSILOPHODON

elongated segment
of hind leg

Camptosaurs

The camptosaurs were a group of ornithischian plant eaters that date from the middle Jurassic to the early Cretaceous. Like many dinosaurs, they had short forelimbs and long, thick hind limbs. They probably were bipedal (upright) runners but dropped to all fours to feed. They may have used their forelimbs to assist in pulling branches to within reach of the mouth. They clipped vegetation with a *short, horny beak* and ground up the plant material with molarlike teeth housed in long, *horse-like jaws.* The lower jaw had an *odd groove,* which suggests to some scientists the possibility that these dinosaurs had a long tongue that might have been used to wrap around vegetation and pull it toward them.

CAMPTOSAURUS   To 20 ft.

Skeletons of *Camptosaurus* (KAMP-toh-SAW-rus) have been found in both North America and Europe. When fully grown, this animal would have weighed about half a ton. It lived during the late Jurassic and early Cretaceous. The camptosaurs are thought to be the ancestors of the larger iguanodons (see next page), which were found later in the Cretaceous.

CAMPTOSAURUS

IGUANODON
To 30 ft.

Named for its supposed resemblance to the modern iguanas, this was the first dinosaur to be described, when Dr. Gideon Mantell brought *Iguanodon* to the world's attention in 1822. Actually, his wife found the fossils, some odd teeth, near Brighton, England. Baron Cuvier, France's leading expert on anatomy, thought the teeth resembled those of a giant iguana, hence the name *Iguanodon* (ih-GWAH-no-don), which means "iguana tooth." Even when more complete skeletons were unearthed, both French and British scientists put the bones together the wrong way — they placed the thumb spike on the nose, like a rhino's horn. *Iguanodon* was restored as though it were a giant lizard shaped like a rhino!

Iguanodon was of great interest to the public because of its size. A full-sized restoration was once used as a dining room by a group of 20 prominent British scientists! Many skeletons have been found and iguanodonts ranged widely over the earth. Males were larger than females and both sexes fed together in herds.

OURANOSAURUS
To 23 ft.

Somewhat like *Spinosaurus* (see p. 38), *Ouranosaurus* (OAR-ahn-oh-SAW-rus) had elongated spines supporting a *finlike structure* on its back, which may have helped it heat up or cool down.

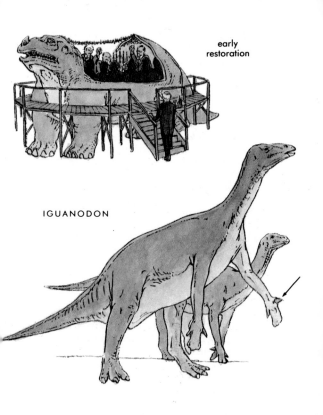

early
restoration

IGUANODON

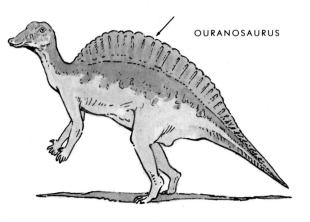

OURANOSAURUS

Hadrosaurs

The many hadrosaur species are known collectively as the duck-billed dinosaurs. Because their *mouths resemble the flattened bills of ducks,* it is not surprising that these large plant eaters were thought to have spent most of their time in the water, feeding on soft vegetation. Like so many other earlier beliefs about dinosaurs, this, too, is a myth. Duck-bills lived in herds in upland areas, and fed on coarse pine needles, fruits, and seeds. If they moved into water, it was probably to escape predators. They clipped vegetation clumps, which they ground up using many rows of flattened teeth. As many as 2,000 teeth could be housed in a single duck-bill! As teeth wore out, they were quickly replaced.

EDMONTOSAURUS   To 43 ft.
Fossils of this large duck-bill have been found in New Jersey, New Mexico, and Canada. Some fossils contain not only the bones but also mummified skin and tendons, providing a very good look at how *Edmontosaurus* (ed-MON-toh-SAW-rus) was structured. Its skin consisted of *fine scales* that did not overlap, as in a lizard or snake.

SAUROLOPHUS   To 30 ft.
Saurolophus (SAW-roh-loh-fuss) had a flattened face with a *small crest* at the rear of the skull. The face had a *flap of skin* between the nostrils and eyes that may have been inflatable. Perhaps this "nose balloon" was used in courtship or to make any calls the animal uttered louder.

broad-beaked
skull

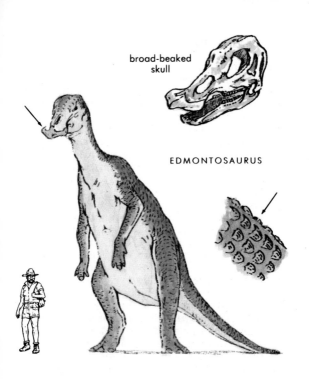

EDMONTOSAURUS

nose balloon
inflated

SAUROLOPHUS

Dinosaur Nesting Behavior

The question of how dinosaurs reproduced and reared their young was once a great mystery. Now the answers are at least partially known. Fossil eggs have been found from several dinosaurs, including the ones we show on this page and on pp. 84–85. Like the birds and crocodiles, to which they were closely related, dinosaurs laid eggs. They also scraped out nests and parents tended their hatchlings. Some dinosaurs nested in colonies, like modern gulls and terns.

MAIASAURUS   To 30 ft.

The name of this Cretaceous dinosaur means "mother lizard," an apt choice since its fossils include eggs, hatchlings, and juveniles as well as adults. A nesting colony of maiasaurs (MAH-ee-uh-sawrs) lived along a river nearly 80 million years ago, in what is now Montana. The adults stood nearly 15 ft. tall and the babies were 1 ft. tall and 3 ft. long at hatching. Clutches of 20 eggs were contained in a mud nest 6 ft. in diameter. Herds of adult and juvenile maiasaurs fed on vegetation. The adults probably protected the young from marauding carnosaurs. Maiasaurs belonged to a group called hadrosaurs (see also p. 78).

MAIASAURUS

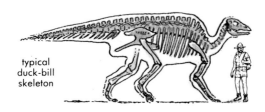

typical
duck-bill
skeleton

Crested Duck-bills

Many duck-bill species had *elaborate crests of bone* on their heads. These bones contained nasal passages and were possibly used to help the dinosaurs make loud trumpeting sounds or detect odors. The odd shapes and unique sounds may have helped duck-bill species recognize each other. An old belief was that the crests stored air while the animal was under water. This is no longer taken seriously.

PARASAUROLOPHUS   To 33 ft.

This dinosaur had a *crest over 3 ft. long* extending beyond its skull. Air had to travel from the nostrils, located at the tip of the snout, all the way up and down the crest before moving to the throat and lungs.

CORYTHOSAURUS   To 33 ft.

The *disklike crest* on this large hadrosaur was most pronounced on males, and smaller in females and juveniles.

LAMBEOSAURUS   To 40 ft.

The crest of this hadrosaur was *almost hatchetlike,* with the blade over the nose and the handle extending beyond the skull.

Each of the three crested hadrosaurs described above lived during the late Cretaceous, in what is now Alberta, Canada. Perhaps they foraged in mixed herds, as African antelopes do today.

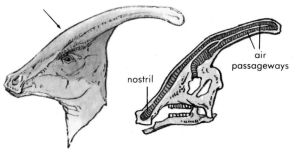

PARASAUROLOPHUS

air passageways

nostril

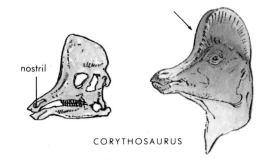

nostril

CORYTHOSAURUS

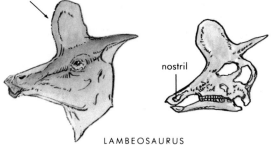

nostril

LAMBEOSAURUS

Bone-headed Dinosaurs

In the late Cretaceous Period there lived an odd group of plant-eating dinosaurs that was characterized by *very dense, bony skulls*, raised in a *domelike shape.* It is not clear exactly which major group of dinosaurs gave rise to the bone-heads. Some scientists believe the bone-heads should be classified as ornithopods, while others believe they should be in their own group.

PACHYCEPHALOSAURUS   To 25 ft.

The rather cumbersome name of this dinosaur means "thick-headed lizard." *Pachycephalosaurus* (PAK-kih-SEFF-ah-loh-SAW-rus) is well named, considering that its *domed bony skull* is 9 in. thick between the tiny brain and outer surface of the skull. The nose and rear of the skull were covered by odd bumps and bony nodules. Many experts now believe that these boneheads used their thick skulls in butting contests, much as bighorn sheep do today. Perhaps male pachycephalosaurs established their dominance by outbutting rivals.

STEGOCERAS   To 6 ft.

This small bone-head has left enough fossils so that scientists can trace the development of its *domed, thick skull.* Males may have had thicker skulls than females, and juveniles had much less bony skulls. The backbone and tail were reinforced by tendons, adding to the strength of *Stegoceras* (steg-GOSS-er-us) as it used its head as a battering ram.

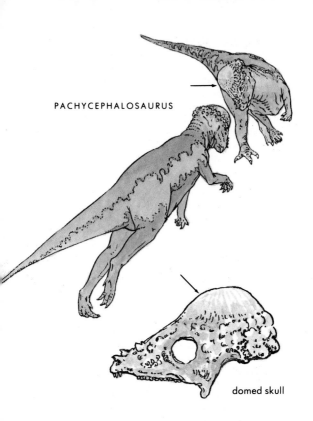

PACHYCEPHALOSAURUS

domed skull

STEGOCERAS

Ankylosaurs

These four-footed dinosaurs of the middle and
late Cretaceous were built along the same lines
as an army tank! Their thick legs supported
husky bodies that were well covered by thick
bony scales, nodules, and spikes. They ate vegetation, clipped with their beaklike mouths.
Should any carnosaur dare provoke or
threaten an ankylosaur (AN-kee-loh-sawr), it
could defend itself by swinging its *long, agile
tail* tipped with a *bony club.* Like today's rhinos, ankylosaurs, though bulky, could move
with surprising speed. All were ornithischians.

EUOPLOCEPHALUS   To 20 ft.

This large ankylosaur from western North
America would easily dwarf a full-sized
automobile. *Euoplocephalus* (YOU-ploh-
SEFF-ah-lus) weighed up to 3 tons. The
skull was very bony and the teeth were
almost tiny.

NODOSAURUS   To 18 ft.

Nodosaurs (NO-doh-sawrs) were less bulky
and possibly less agile than their larger relatives, the ankylosaurs. They lacked the
club-tipped tail but had *armorlike skin* over
part of their backs. Some had large spikes
along their sides. Nodosaurs are less well
known than ankylosaurs.

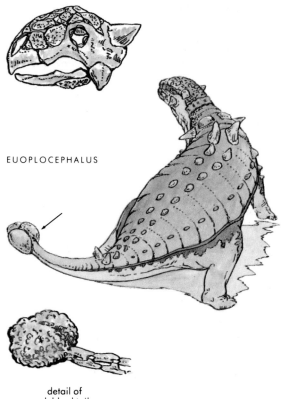

EUOPLOCEPHALUS

detail of
clubbed tail

NODOSAURUS

PROTOCERATOPS

To 6 ft.

Just as the maiasaurs (see pp. 76–77) nested in Montana, so did these small four-legged dinosaurs in Outer Mongolia. The nests, eggs, and young of *Protoceratops* (PROH-toh-SAIR-ah-tops) were discovered in 1922 during an historic expedition of scientists from the American Museum of Natural History. These eggs were the first dinosaur eggs ever discovered. In a remote area of the Gobi Desert, known as "Flaming Cliffs" for its striking red colors, were found dozens of *Protoceratops* skeletons of all ages, along with many eggs, some of which were still arranged in circular patterns in their fossilized nests. Like the maiasaurs, these small dinosaurs may have gathered in colonies to reproduce. *Protoceratops* lived in the mid-Cretaceous and was one of the first of the ceratopsid (SAIR-ah-TOP-sid) dinosaurs (see next two pages). Its head, with a sharp beak and small teeth, tapered into a *prominent neck shield.* This dinosaur ate only plants.

PSITTACOSAURUS

To 6½ ft.

This small dinosaur from the mid-Cretaceous had a body much like that of an ornithopod, with grasping forelimbs and long, strong hind limbs for rearing up. However, its *parrotlike beak* indicates its kinship to *Protoceratops* and the other ceratopsids.

male

PROTOCERATOPS

female
at nest

PSITTACOSAURUS

Ceratopsids

Fossils of these rhinoceros-like dinosaurs of the late Cretaceous are found widely in western North America. They were abundant and many species existed. All were four-legged and husky, and each species had a *conspicuous bony frill* extending from behind its eyes, shielding its neck and shoulder region. Varying arrangements of *spikes and horns* protruded from the neck shield and facial bones. All ceratopsids were vegetarians. Though they resembled modern rhinos of the African plains, and could gallop as rhinos do, these dinosaurs probably inhabited forests, browsing on tree leaves.

MONOCLONIUS To 18 ft.

Named for the *single prominent horn* above its nasal area, this dinosaur had a *short neck shield* with bony knobs along the rim. *Monoclonius* (MOH-no-KLO-nee-us) may have used the horn both as a defense against carnosaurs and against territorial rivals.

STYRACOSAURUS To 18 ft.

This ceratopsid also had a *large nasal horn* but had a neck shield from which radiated *long spikes.* Perhaps *Styracosaurus* (STY-rah-koh-SAW-rus) swung its head vigorously from side to side when attacked by a carnosaur.

CHASMOSAURUS To 17 ft.

The *neck shield* of this dinosaur was quite elongated. *Chasmosaurus* (KAZ-moh-SAW-rus) had a *small nasal horn* plus a *prominent horn above each eye.* It could rear up on its hind legs and face an opponent or predator, displaying its neck frill to the fullest. Some scientists believe the neck frills of ceratopsids were brightly colored and were used for courtship or threat displays as well as protection.

MONOCLONIUS

STYRACOSAURUS

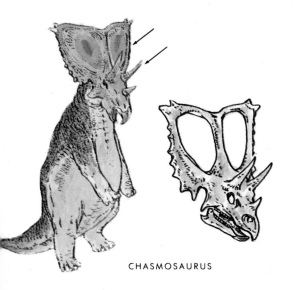

CHASMOSAURUS

TRICERATOPS   To 30 ft.

During the late Cretaceous, the 6-ton "three-horned face," as the name *Triceratops* (try-SEER-ah-tops) means, galloped in abundance over what is now the American West. This was one of the last of the dinosaurs — quite possibly *the* last species to exist. The long horns above each eye measure up to 3 ft. in length but may have been longer. All that remains are bony cores, but in life each horn may have been covered by additional material, as in modern sheep and goats. A herd of *Triceratops* would have been no easy prey for a hungry *Tyrannosaurus.* Like African rhinos today, an adult *Triceratops* was able to run from danger or face it with a strong offense. Fossil locations show that these dinosaurs probably inhabited forests of redwoods and other tall trees. They ate only plant food, which they cropped with their beaklike mouths and ground up with their flattened, molarlike teeth.

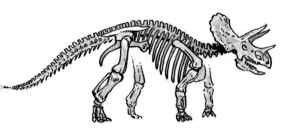

bird-hipped
skeleton

TRICERATOPS

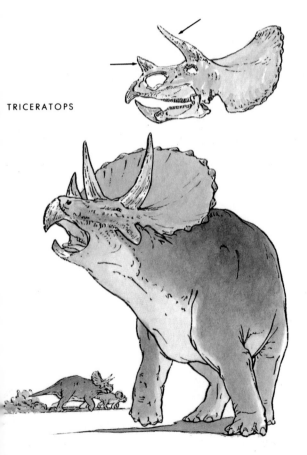

Crocodilians

Crocodiles and alligators are "modern" reptiles in that they are still with us. However, as a group, the crocodilians date back to the Triassic. The largest crocodiles ever to exist were contemporaries with dinosaurs. Crocodilians are most definitely not dinosaurs, though both groups of animals do share a common ancestor, a thecodont (see p. 24). Crocodiles have changed little over their millions of years on the planet. All are aquatic carnivores, with powerful tails used in swimming, and long jaws armed with sharp teeth.

PROTOSUCHUS   To 3½ ft.

This little animal was one of the first crocodilians. Its fossils are found in the American Southwest, and date from the late Triassic Period. *Protosuchus* (PROH-toh-soo-kus) had *longer legs* and a *shorter skull* than modern crocodiles. Like modern members of its group, it had *thickened skin* protecting its back.

METRIORHYNCHUS   To 10 ft.

This crocodile was unusual because it had *paddle-like flippers* rather than legs, and a *whale-like tail.* These characteristics indicate that it was totally aquatic. It probably pursued fish, which it captured with its slender, toothy snout. Another unusual feature was the *total lack of armor* on the skin. *Metriorhynchus* (meh-TREE-oh-RINK-us) lived in the Jurassic Period.

DEINOSUCHUS   To 50 ft.

Imagine a crocodile that extends almost from the pitcher's mound to home plate! *Deinosuchus* (DY-no-SOO-kus), whose name means "terrible crocodile," was just such a creature. This immense animal, the largest crocodile known, lived in the late Cretaceous Period. It was quite capable of devouring dinosaurs, and may have grabbed them as they came to the water's edge to drink. Fossils come from Texas, a state known for bigness.

skull
(top view)

skull
(profile)

PROTOSUCHUS

METRIORHYNCHUS

DEINOSUCHUS

Lizards, Snakes, and Turtles

Besides crocodilians, there are three other major groups of reptiles alive today. Each group traces its roots back to the Mesozoic Era. Lizards evolved in the later part of the Triassic, and are thriving today, with 6,000 species. Most of them live in warm regions such as rain forests and deserts. Snakes do not appear in the fossil record until the late Cretaceous, and are in many respects similar to lizards, though they lack limbs. The most ancient snakes are the huge constrictors, whose modern species include the pythons and anaconda. Turtles date back to the Triassic and differ from both dinosaurs and other modern reptiles in that their ancestor is not a thecodont (see p. 24). Turtles evolved from an early group of stem reptiles before the Mesozoic began.

MOSASAUR To 30 ft.

Mosasaurs (MOH-zah-sawrs) were large aquatic lizards of the Cretaceous. *Tylosaurus,* shown here, lived in a sea that covered Kansas 70 million years ago. The *paddle-like feet* and *long tail* made mosasaurs efficient swimmers.

PYTHON To 30 ft., or more

These thick-bodied snakes kill their prey by constriction, or squeezing, which prevents their victims from breathing. The reticulated python, shown here, is alive today, and is found in southeast Asia. It can reach a length of 33 ft. Fossil pythons appear quite similar.

ARCHELON To 12 ft.

Archelon (AR-kee-lon) was a large sea turtle of the Cretaceous. It lived in a vast inland sea covering what is now South Dakota, where its fossils were found. The name means "ruler turtle," a reference to its large size.

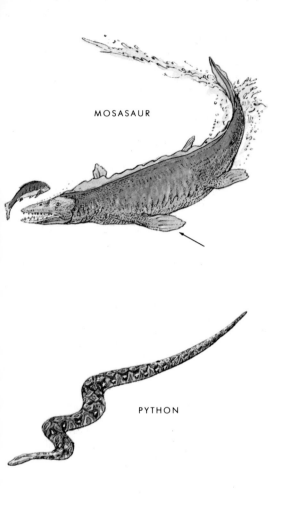

MOSASAUR

PYTHON

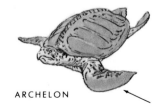

ARCHELON

Plesiosaurs

During the Jurassic and Cretaceous periods these large marine reptiles (which were *not* dinosaurs) inhabited the world's oceans. All plesiosaurs (PLEE-see-oh-sawrs) had *paddle-like fins*, rather like those of modern sea turtles. Plesiosaurs may have come ashore to lay eggs. Many plesiosaurs had long necks. All probably were active predators, feeding on fish.

PLESIOSAURUS   To 10 ft.

This was one of the first of the plesiosaurs, living in the early Jurassic. As in most plesiosaurs, the *long neck* contained many vertebrae. This would have made the neck quite flexible, an aid in capturing swift fish.

ELASMOSAURUS   To 47 ft.

In the late Cretaceous, western North America was largely covered by a vast inland sea, the home of *Elasmosaurus* (ee-lass-moh-SAW-rus), this ancient "sea serpent." Its highly flexible neck contained about 70 vertebrae, and measured 25 ft. long. The jaws were filled with sharp teeth.

KRONOSAURUS   To 56 ft.

This huge plesiosaur swam in seas around Australia during the early Cretaceous. *Kronosaurus* (KROH-no-SAW-rus) was rather similar to a modern sperm whale, with *huge jaws* lined with *conical teeth.* Though it could dive deeply, it was nonetheless a reptile, and needed to surface to breathe air.

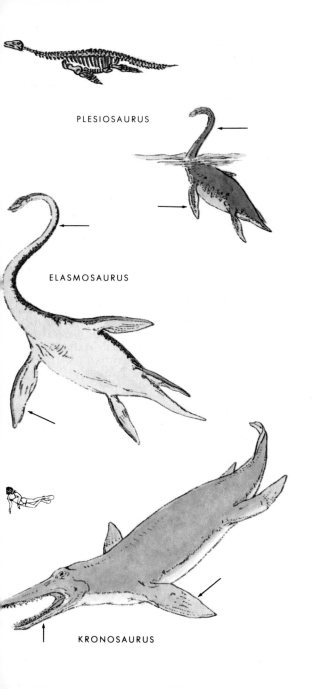

PLESIOSAURUS

ELASMOSAURUS

KRONOSAURUS

Ichthyosaurs

The name ichthyosaur (ICK-thee-oh-sawr) means "fish-lizard," a good description of these aquatic reptiles of the Mesozoic Era. They closely resembled fish in body form, though they breathed air, as do all reptiles. Fossils indicate that ichthyosaurs gave birth to live young.

ICHTHYOSAURUS To 10 ft.

This swift, streamlined animal could swim efficiently in pursuit of fish. Its jaws were *elongated* and lined with sharp teeth. Notice how similar ichthyosaurs were to porpoises, though their reptilian brains were not nearly as large as those of the aquatic mammals.

SHONISAURUS To 50 ft.

At 40 tons, with a 10-ft.-long skull, and eyeballs fully 1 ft. in diameter, this was by far the largest of the ichthyosaurs. *Shonisaurus* (SHOW-nee-SAW-rus) was similar to *Kronosaurus* (a plesiosaur) in general anatomy but lived much earlier, in the Triassic Period. *Shonisaurus* may well have been the largest creature of the Triassic.

Placodonts

These early aquatic reptiles resembled modern marine iguanas such as the lizards found on the Galápagos Islands.

PLACODUS To 6 ft.

Using its long tail for propulsion, this husky placodont (PLAY-koh-dahnt) would dive in search of clams and mussels, which it would dig out with its *blunt, peglike teeth.*

modern porpoise, for comparison

ICHTHYOSAURUS

SHONISAURUS

peglike teeth

crushing teeth

PLACODUS

Pterosaurs

During the time of the dinosaurs there were two groups of flying vertebrates, the birds and the pterosaurs. Pterosaurs (TERR-oh-sawrs) were reptiles whose ancestors were similar to those of dinosaurs. Pterosaurs differed from birds in that their wing was a *large membrane of skin*, supported by a *single elongated finger* (their other name, *pterodactyl*, means "wing-finger"). Pterosaurs were a diverse group, including sparrow-sized species as well as the largest flying creatures ever known. Because of the energy demands of flight, they may have been warm-blooded, and may have been covered by fine fur. Pterosaurs evolved before birds, and were in the skies throughout the Mesozoic Era, but all became extinct at the end of the Cretaceous.

RAMPHORHYNCHUS   Wingspan 5 ft.
This sharp-toothed pterosaur captured fish. It lived during the Jurassic, in what is now Bavaria in West Germany. *Ramphorhyncus* (RAM-foh-RINK-us) had a *long, spearlike tail,* used as a rudder in steering.

PTERANODON   Wingspan 23 ft.
Soaring like an ancient albatross over Cretaceous seas that covered what is now Kansas and Texas, the majestic *Pteranodon* (TERR-an-oh-don) hunted large fish. Scientists estimate that this flying dinosaur could glide at speeds of up to 25 miles per hour. The *long crest* on its head may have been used as a rudder, for steering.

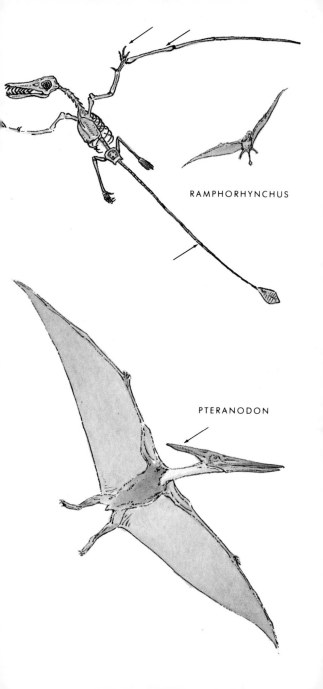

RAMPHORHYNCHUS

PTERANODON

QUETZALCOATLUS   Wingspan 36–50 ft.

This pterosaur is the largest flying verte-brate known. Its fossils come from Big Bend National Park, Texas. With its *broad wings*, *Quetzalcoatlus* (KET-sahl-COAT-luss) must have soared like a modern glider aircraft, perhaps in search of the remains of huge sauropods upon which it fed, much as vultures feed on carcasses of elephants and other animals today.

DIMORPHODON   Wingspan 5 ft.

Present early in the Jurassic, *Dimorphodon* (dy-MOR-foh-don) may have pursued its prey by running after it on its long legs. Like all pterosaurs, it could also fly well, flapping its wings with the skill of a modern bird or bat.

PTERODAUSTRO   Wingspan 4½ ft.

A most unusual pterosaur, this creature had a lower jaw lined with *elongate comb-like teeth* that probably filtered minute planktonic organisms from water, as the bill of a modern flamingo does. *Pterodaus-tro* (TERR-oh-DASS-tro) lived during the early Cretaceous, in what is now Argentina.

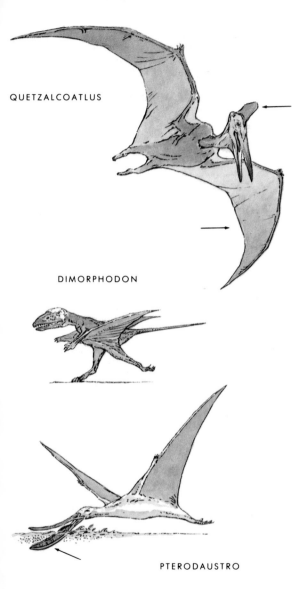

QUETZALCOATLUS

DIMORPHODON

PTERODAUSTRO

comblike jaw
for filtering food

Cretaceous Birds

Though birds first evolved from small coelurosaur dinosaurs during the Jurassic (see p. 48), by the Cretaceous Period some birds hardly resembled their Jurassic ancestors. Two of these more "modern" birds lived along the coast of a vast sea that covered much of what is now the midwestern part of the United States.

HESPERORNIS   To 5 ft.

Resembling a large loon, *Hesperornis* (HESS-per-OAR-nis) was a diving bird that inhabited lakes and seacoasts. It differed from loons in that it had a *fully toothed beak* and could not fly. Its life must have been spent largely on water, diving deeply for fish. Its legs were placed *far back*, a useful position for powerful diving, and its feet were impressively large, and probably webbed. The name *Hesperornis* means "western bird."

ICHTHYORNIS   To 1 ft.

Flying above the seas where *Hesperornis* dove was *Ichthyornis* (ICK-thee-OAR-nis), whose name means "fish-eating bird." This species more closely resembled a modern bird than *Hesperornis,* and was a powerful flyer. It probably resembled a modern gull or a big, plump tern, though it has also been compared with puffins. Unlike modern birds, it had a *fully toothed bill,* probably an adaptation for capturing slippery fish.

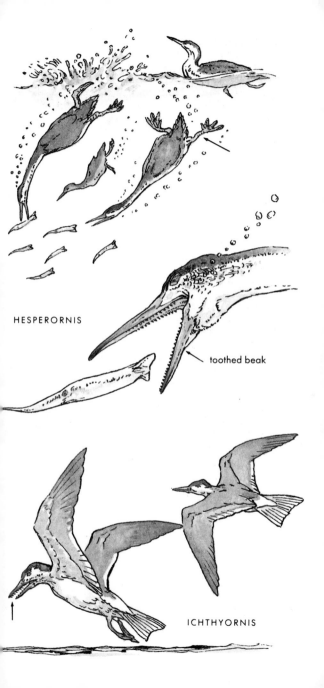

HESPERORNIS

toothed beak

ICHTHYORNIS

The End of the Dinosaurs

Did dinosaurs go out with a bang or a whimper? Actually, they probably did both. The fossil record indicates that most dinosaurs had already become extinct before the end of the Cretaceous Period. Dinosaurs were becoming gradually less abundant and diverse long before they finally disappeared. The climate was changing, becoming more temperate, and perhaps most species failed to adapt to the changes. However, a sudden and large-scale extinction that took place at the very end of the Cretaceous, which affected not only dinosaurs but most other kinds of animals, including many marine species, suggests that some sweeping, catastrophic event killed off all the

animals at once. Evidence from geology indicates that such an event did, in fact, occur. It
is possible that an asteroid (a small, planetlike
body about 5—6 miles in diameter) or a comet
collided with the earth 65 million years ago,
causing a severe and sudden climatic change.

Scientists differ as to the effects of such a
cosmic collision: Most say that the earth got
much darker and cooler, but some argue that
the earth suddenly got warmer. In either case,
conditions were no longer suitable for most
animals that had thrived during the Cretaceous Period, so they died off in large numbers. Large-scale volcanic activity may also
have caused a change in climate similar to
that triggered by the supposed cosmic collision.

Big Bad Birds

The end of the Cretaceous Period and the extinction of the great dinosaurs left a void. Soon the mammals evolved and replaced the giant reptiles. However, for a relatively brief time at the beginning of the Cenozoic Era (see p. 12), some rather large, predatory birds evolved. These big birds chased, captured, and fed on the little 'mammals that lived during the Mesozoic.

DIATRYMA To 6 ft. tall

This huge predatory bird roamed the North American plains 50 million years ago. With an *immense hawklike bill* and powerful running legs, *Diatryma* (DY-ah-TRY-mah) must have been one of the largest carnivores of its time.

PHORUSRHACOS To 6 ft. tall

As *Diatryma* terrorized the diminutive mammals of North America, so did *Phorusrhacos* (FOR-russ-HOCK-us) in South America. This giant bird lived about 20 million years ago, in what is now Argentina and Chile. Though both *Diatryma* and *Phorusrhacos* were very effective predators of their time, each was a far cry from their carnosaur predecessors.

DINORNIS To 11½ ft. tall

Though big, this bird was harmless. *Dinornis* (DIN-oar-nis) belonged to a group of plant-eating birds called moas, all of which lived on New Zealand. These birds were overhunted by the Maoris of New Zealand. Most of the moas became extinct only about 400 years ago. The only surviving moas are the flightless kiwis, close relatives of *Dinornis*. Kiwis are New Zealand's national bird.

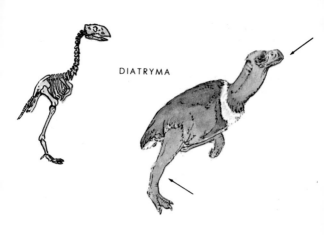

DIATRYMA

PHORUSRHACOS

DINORNIS

kiwi,
for comparison

Mammal-like Reptiles

Both dinosaurs and mammals evolved from ancient reptiles, but the reptiles that gave rise to mammals were quite distinct from those that were ancestors to dinosaurs. Mammals descended from a diverse group of creatures known as mammal-like reptiles because their skull bones, jaws, and teeth bear a close similarity to those of mammals. Modern mammals have a body covering of hair and suckle their young with milk, but we are uncertain as to when these features evolved, as they do not leave fossils. Mammal-like reptiles lived before dinosaurs, in the Permian Period (see p. 12), and survived through much of the Triassic. They eventually became extinct, but were survived by the first true mammals.

PELYCOSAURS   To 11 ft.

Among the first mammal-like reptiles was a group in which some species had *long spines* projecting from their vertebral columns. When these animals were alive, a membrane of skin enclosed the spines, giving the animals a *sail-backed* appearance. No one knows why such a structure was present, but it may have been a solar panel, absorbing and radiating heat to help the animal warm up or cool down.

Two well-known pelycosaurs (PELL-eh-koh-sawrs) are shown here. *Dimetrodon* was a carnivore, among the largest of its time. It had formidable *slashing teeth*. *Edaphosaurus* was a small-headed plant eater, with peglike teeth.

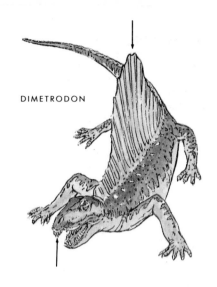

DIMETRODON

PELYCOSAUR

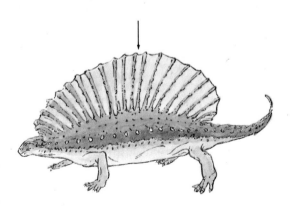

EDAPHOSAURUS

Therapsids

As these mammal-like reptiles evolved, they
became increasingly similar to true mammals.

MOSCHOPS   To 8 ft.

Imagine a toad about the size of a sedan
and you get some idea of a *Moschops*
(MOSS-kops). This lumbering plant eater
belonged to a group called the dinocephali-
ans (DY-no-seff-FAY-lee-ans). As hard as it
may be to believe, herds of these reptiles
grazed what is now South Africa during the
mid-Permian Period.

LYSTROSAURUS   To 3 ft.

Fossils of this small, mammal-like reptile
have been found in India, South Africa,
China, and Antarctica. The wide distribution of this small, land-dwelling animal
helps support the idea that the earth's continents were once joined in one large land
mass back in the Permian Period. *Lystrosaurus* (LISS-troh-SAW-rus) was a dicyno-
dont, meaning "double dog-tooth," a
reference to its two upper canine teeth.
Although it had canines, this reptile ate
only plants. It may have used the sharp
canines to defend itself.

CYNOGNATHUS   To 5 ft.

Though it is considered a reptile, *Cynognathus* (whose name means "dog-jawed") was
a carnivore and probably would look very
much like a primitive wolf. It belonged to a
group called the theriodonts, meaning
"beast-toothed." The skull and teeth of
Cynognathus (SIN-og-nath-us) were almost
like those of a modern mammal, and it may
have been warm-blooded and covered by
fur. *Cynognathus* lived in the mid-Triassic.
Its limbs and overall body shape were similar to those of true mammals, which are,
indeed, evolved from advanced theriodonts.

MOSCHOPS

LYSTROSAURUS

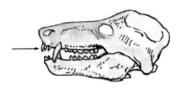

CYNOGNATHUS

Early Cenozoic Mammals

Mammals have a rich fossil history. Many fossils of the ancestors of horses, elephants, camels, and lions of today have been discovered. Here are a few examples of small furred creatures that lived very long ago. Modern mammals trace their genetic roots to these animals.

HYRACOTHERIUM   To 2 ft.

A horse the size of a terrier? Indeed, as odd as it may seem, the first horse was a dainty, five-toed animal that bore faint resemblance to the single-toed thoroughbreds of today. Horses of many species lived during the Cenozoic, but little *Hyracotherium* (hi-RACK-oh-thee-ree-um), also called *Eohippus*, the "dawn horse," was the first. It lived in North America, where it fed on leaves.

MOERITHERIUM   To 5 ft.

This husky, sheep-sized creature was the ancestor of the proboscideans, or elephants. Its *short snout* gave little indication of the long, flexible trunk that would eventually characterize its descendants. Fossils of *Moeritherium* (MORE-ih-THEER-ee-um) come from northern Africa.

PHENACODUS   To 4 ft.

This animal is about the size of a goat, to which it is very distantly related. *Phenacodus* (FEEN-ah-koh-dus), was a condylarth, a member of the group from which all hoofed or ungulate mammals evolved. *Phenacodus* fed on plants and was the first true hoofed mammal. Its fossils come from Europe and North America.

PATRIOFELIS   To 6 ft.

Just as different types of plant-eating mammals developed, so did different types of meat eaters. *Patriofelis* (pah-TREE-oh-FEE-liss) was an early creodont, a member of the group that gave rise to bears, cats, dogs, and other carnivores. It hunted its prey in North America nearly 60 million years ago.

HYRACOTHERIUM

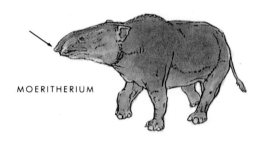

MOERITHERIUM

PHENACODUS

PATRIOFELIS

Early Mammalian Giants

UINTATHERIUM   To 10 ft.

This odd-looking creature was an ambly-pod, a slow-moving plant eater that roamed in the American West in the early Cenozoic. Its grotesque skull, with *knobby projections* and *long canine teeth*, made *Uintatherium* (YOU-in-tah-THEER-ee-um) a dangerous animal to challenge.

PLATYBELODON   To 12 ft.

One of the more unusual of the elephants, *Platybelodon* (PLAT-ih-BELL-oh-don) is often called the "shovel-tusker." Its unique *lower jaw* probably was useful for scooping up plants. It lived in North America and Asia during the mid-Cenozoic.

PARACERATHERIUM   To 26 ft.

This early rhinoceros lacked a horn on its face. It hardly needed any, considering its immense size — it stood 18 ft. tall at the shoulder! Like the sauropods of the Meso-zoic, *Paraceratherium* (pah-rah-SEER-ah-THEER-ee-um) supported its bulk on a diet of leaves, cropped from the crowns of tall trees. Among the mammals, only the big-gest whales are larger. Fossils of *Paracer-atherium* were found in Asia.

MEGISTOTHERIUM   To 18 ft.

A trip to northern Africa during the mid-Cenozoic could be risky, because that is where *Megistotherium* (meh-JISS-toe-THEER-ee-um), the largest mammalian car-nivore ever known, roamed in search of prey. It probably fed on elephants and similar-sized creatures. It weighed nearly a ton, and had a skull twice as large as a grizzly bear's.

UINTATHERIUM

PLATYBELODON

PARACERATHERIUM

MEGISTOTHERIUM

South American Giants

Several impressively large mammals lived in South America just prior to and during the Ice Age.

TOXODON To 10 ft.

A *Toxodon* (TOCK-so-don) was a lumbering plant-eating beast that resembled a combination of a rhino and a pig. Its bulk was probably its major protection. *Toxodon* snipped off leaves with its sharp incisor teeth and ground them up with its large molars. It belonged to a group of hoofed mammals called the notoungulates, found only in South America.

GLYPTODON To 10 ft.

Related to the armadillos, *Glyptodon* (GLIP-toe-don) looked like a huge mammalian tortoise. Protected by its *dense bony covering*, it plodded along, munching plants. If irritated, it could swing its *clublike* tail. Compare it with the ankylosaurs (see pp. 82–83).

MEGATHERIUM To 20 ft.

Appropriately called the giant ground sloth, *Megatherium* (MEG-gah-THEER-ee-um) could rear up on its hind legs to reach tree-top vegetation. Though quite large, it bore a close similarity to today's much smaller tree sloths. This fact influenced Charles Darwin to consider the idea of evolution.

TOXODON

GLYPTODON

three-toed sloth,
for comparison

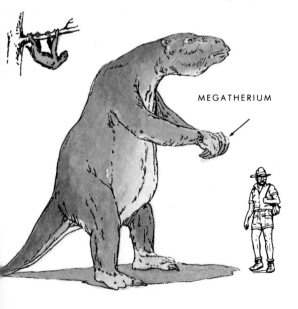

MEGATHERIUM

Ice-Age Mammals

Beginning about two million years ago and ending only 20,000 years ago, great sheets of glacial ice moved periodically from far northern latitudes to cover North America and Europe, creating a time of great cold known as the Ice Age. Several unique mammals roamed over the barren terrain.

WOOLLY MAMMOTH   To 10 ft. tall
The *shaggy fur* and extremely *long, curved tusks* identify this Ice-Age elephant. In Russia, frozen woolly mammoths have been discovered, providing us with detailed looks at the fur and skin. Some scientists even tasted the meat, which had been frozen for thousands of years. It didn't taste very good.

WOOLLY RHINOCEROS   To 10 ft.
Bulk seems to be one way for animals to protect themselves against cold. This animal had almost the bulk of a modern elephant. Like the preceding species, it was also covered by *shaggy fur.* Its *horn* measured just over 6 ft. in length.

IRISH ELK   To 15 ft.
This huge deer had an *immense antler rack* that measured 11 ft. across from tip to tip. The elk probably used its wide antler rack to threaten rivals.

SMILODON   To 6 ft.
The "saber-toothed cat" was most notable for its *8-in.-long upper canine teeth,* undoubtedly used to bring down large prey such as ground sloths.

WOOLLY MAMMOTH

WOOLLY
RHINOCEROS

IRISH ELK

SMILODON

Human Ancestors

Given the earth's long history, humans are a recent species. Our ancestors originated in Africa, probably around six million years ago. Fossil remains tell us that there were several species of hominids that preceded our own species, *Homo sapiens.*

AUSTRALOPITHECUS AFARENSIS　To 3½ ft.
This small hominid is best known as the famous fossil "Lucy," a skeleton that is 40% complete. "Lucy" shows that *afarensis* (ah-FAR-en-sis) walked fully upright, as we do. Fossil footprints have also been found and they are no different from our own. Judging from the position of the bones in her skull, Lucy's face would have somewhat resembled that of a chimpanzee. Her brain was probably only about one-third as large as ours. Lucy and her family lived about three and a half million years ago, in east Africa.

PARANTHROPUS BOISEI　　　To 4½ ft.
Larger and more robust than little *afarensis, Paranthropus* (PAIR-an-THROW-puss) hominids inhabited east Africa in groups until about one and a half million years ago. Their large jaws and teeth indicate that they ate coarse plant material.

HOMO ERECTUS　　　　　　To 5 ft.
Homo erectus (hoe-moh ee-RECK-tus) evolved in Africa, but spread over Europe and Asia. Fossils show that these hominids persisted until about 500,000 years ago. They lived in cooperative groups that made and used tools, and probably used fire to cook. Their brain size was nearly three-fourths that of modern humans. Our species is probably a direct descendent of *Homo erectus.*

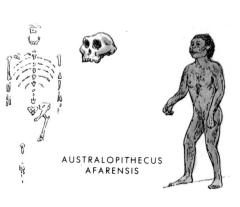

AUSTRALOPITHECUS
AFARENSIS

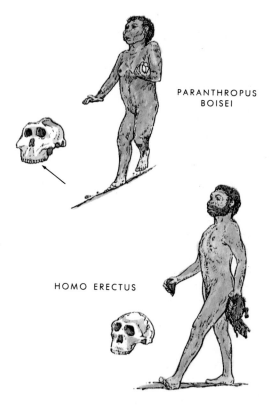

PARANTHROPUS
BOISEI

HOMO ERECTUS

Living Fossils

Some plants and animals that are alive today have long histories that can be traced in the fossil record of ancient rocks.

COCKROACH To 6 in.

Among the most common house pests, cockroaches are the oldest, dating back to the Carboniferous, nearly 350 million years ago. Today there are between 3,000 and 4,000 species. Many have scarcely changed from the time when these nocturnal insects first scurried through primeval undergrowth, long before the dinosaurs.

HORSESHOE CRAB To 2 ft.

This animal is more closely related to ancient sea scorpions than to the crabs we eat. Commonly seen along the shores of East Coast seas, the horseshoe crab has barely changed in appearance for 210 million years. Dinosaurs probably gazed at horseshoe crabs along the seashore, just as beachcombers do today.

CHAMBERED NAUTILUS To 1½ ft.

Ancestors of this mollusk preyed on the earliest fishes in the Paleozoic. These animals of deep Pacific waters are related to squids. Along with the squids and octopuses, nautiluses belong to a group of mollusks called cephalopods (SEFF-ah-loh-pods), meaning "head-foot." Nautiluses have many arms around their head, which contains eyes very much like our own.

LINGULA

Lingula is a brachiopod, a kind of animal that resembles clams but is not closely related to them. Most brachiopods lived before the dinosaurs and most are extinct, but *Lingula* is one of the few exceptions. Its ancestors from the early Paleozoic looked nearly identical. Brachiopods fed by opening their shells and capturing tiny food with a long, tentacle-like organ. *Lingula* lives burrowed in the ocean floor, anchored by its long stalk and protected within its clamlike shell.

fossil

COCKROACH

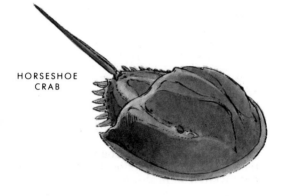

HORSESHOE
CRAB

CHAMBERED
NAUTILUS

LINGULA

GINKGO

This common tree of city streets appears in fossils from the late Paleozoic onward. Ginkgos abounded during the time of the dinosaurs. They are ancient relatives of conifers. Growing to heights of 100 ft., ginkgos are indeed stately links to the past.

COELOCANTH

This 5-ft.-long fish of deep Indian Ocean waters was long believed to be extinct, until it was rediscovered in 1938. It is a lobe-finned fish, with strong bones and muscles supporting its fins. It is closely related to the early fish (see p. 24) that gave rise to amphibians (frogs, toads, and salamanders).

TUATARA

Although it looks much like a large, chunky lizard, the tuatara is in fact not a lizard at all. It is the only surviving member of a group called the rhynchocephalians ("beak-heads") that were abundant during the Mesozoic Era. Tuataras are found only in New Zealand.

OPOSSUM

Opossums are familiar inhabitants of woodlands and frequent victims of automobiles. Their ancestors, which looked scarcely different, fell prey to carnivorous dinosaurs in the late Mesozoic. Opossums are marsupials — they give birth to tiny young that are nurtured in a pouch on the mother's abdomen.

GINKGO

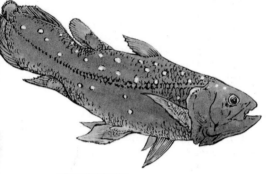

COELOCANTH

TUATARA

OPOSSUM

DINOSAUROID — "DINOSAUR PERSON"

What if dinosaurs had not become extinct and mammals had not inherited the earth? Could intelligent creatures such as ourselves have evolved from dinosaurs? Recently a paleontologist and an artist considered these questions. They suggested that one group of dinosaurs, had they survived, might have eventually evolved intelligence.

In the late Cretaceous Period lived a dinosaur named *Troodon* (see pp. 44–45). This creature, slightly over 6 ft. tall, had a relatively large brain, for a dinosaur. It stood fully upright, which left its arms free to gather food and explore its surroundings. *Troodon* probably hunted small mammals and other swift prey and may have been a very cunning little dinosaur. Given millions of years of evolution, pehaps it would have become "Dinosauroid," an intelligent dinosaur. We'll never know.

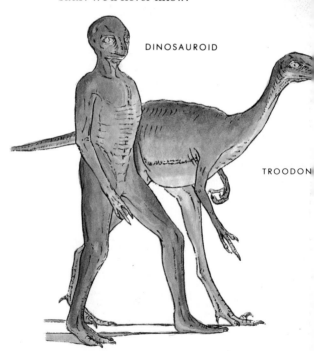

DINOSAUROID

TROODON

Index